The Gamesters' Handbook 3

A new anthology of games for teachers, organisational consultants and managers, families, and group leaders of all kinds, to promote achievement and empower learners.

Donna Brandes ◇ **John Norris**

Games are for everyone

Stanley Thornes (Publishers) Ltd

First published in 1998 by:
Stanley Thornes (Publishers) Ltd
Ellenborough House
Wellington Street
CHELTENHAM GL50 1YW
England

98 99 00 01 02 / 10 9 8 7 6 5 4 3 2 1

A catalogue record for this book is available from the British Library.

ISBN 0-7487-3504-6

Printed and bound in Great Britain by Redwood Books, Trowbridge, Wiltshire

Typeset by Columns Design Ltd., Reading
Illustrated by Matt Marchment (except pp. 99, 123 by Anne Lee)

Contents

Dedication

To all those Gamesters out there who see so clearly how games can enrich the lives of their students, their families and friends, their colleagues, and themselves.

Break away from the crowd

Acknowledgments

Perhaps this page isn't fascinating to anyone except those being acknowledged. However, we would never forgive ourselves if we didn't say thank you to all the people who supported us. Since John is in England, and I am in Western Australia, our lists are pretty separate, and so they appear below.

Donna:

A heartfelt thank you to John Norris, for his courage, creativity, and cheerfulness. I don't think I would have had the stamina and persistence to gather and write this whole anthology myself. To Helen Norris, his wife, and their children, and to John's colleagues and students at Hinchingbrooke School who contributed games.

To Peter Burton of Stanley Thornes (Publishers) Ltd. Thank you for commissioning the book and for being patient in the rough spots.

To Jan Slattery for her tireless typing and to Greg Winn for his kind contribution towards the completion of the book.

To my sons, and their partners, who always support me in so many ways.

To my dear friend and colleague, Tony Harris, for his constancy, his contribution, and his deep commitment to SCL and all it stands for.

To Paul and Sharon Ginnis for their input and their loyalty, and to Ted Harvey for his continued help.

To Gemma Lawlor and John Eaton for remaining loyal RASCLS for all these years, and for contributing their time and their games.

To David Setchell, whom I've never met, but who kept us electronically together and gave a great deal of time and energy to supporting us.

To Jodi Berens, Sarah Carver, and Sue Richardson, RASCLS extraordinaire, who each contributed in their own way to this book.

To Murray White for his willingness to contribute.

To all the people whose names are listed on the games as sources, for their generosity of time and their energy and enthusiasm for this project, including the students from Hinchingbrooke School, and from Harvey Agricultural High School.

To Ian Hunter, for coming in with enthusiasm to complete this project.

John acknowledges …

Helen Norris, for her support, encouragement and ideas.

Jenny and Georgina Norris, for keeping me in touch with reality.

Donna Brandes, for being an excellent mentor and teacher.

David Setchell, for e-mail, humour, efficiency and snooker.

Carolyn Price, for fax and professionalism.

Pauline Maskell, for self-esteem.

Rosemary Carrington, for insights.

Ann Duff, for Big Boss.

Hinchingbrooke students, for support and creativity.

Introduction

A Wise Man said: "There are two kinds of people in this world: Those who think there are two kinds of people, and those who don't."

When we're talking about games, there are basically two kinds of people in the world:

Type I

Those who love games, who find them challenging, stimulating, growthful, and just plain fun. This type does not need an excuse to play; they recognise that play is as important in life as work, and absolutely necessary for healthy living. They may choose sporty type games, such as Golf or Tennis, intellectual games such as Scrabble or Chess, or party games such as Charades or Pictionary. They may make games of one sort or another the focus of their lives, perhaps even becoming professional and earning their living through disciplined play. Others look forward to games as their favourite form of relaxation.

Type II

Those who hate and detest games. This type may never have enjoyed playing for various reasons, perhaps stemming from childhood experiences, or else have been taught/conditioned to believe that grown-ups don't play. They find games at best embarrassing, and at worst, soul-destroying and torturous. They won't join in, or only under duress, feeling, 'I might make a fool of myself'. They shun parties which end in Charades at midnight, while the Die-Hard Gamesters come along eagerly and never want to go home. Others in the I–Hate–Games category simply consider play a waste of precious time.

Sometimes, a Type II can turn into a Type I later in life, if they become, for instance, part of a group where it is perfectly safe to play without embarrassment, and where there is little risk of making a fool of themselves, since everyone else is clearly enjoying play, and not out to humiliate them.

There is a blurred definition between work and play in any case. I like to think that work is no different to play if you love it, similarly, play is hard work if you are competing, or if you hate it. For instance, for me, gardening is sheer drudgery, while I thoroughly enjoy writing and cooking. Others find gardening a balm for their souls, and would never go into the kitchen or sit at a computer if they could help it.

Type III

In the past few decades a new type has emerged, and although there may have been individual examples of Type III in the past, such as teachers who used spelling competitions to add excitement to onerous spelling lessons; it is only recently that the purposeful and deliberate use of games for teaching and training has become popular.

A Type III person realises that games are not only fun, but can be experientially educational. Business organisations, even of the most prestigious variety, now routinely employ consultants who initiate games designed for team-building, personal development, professional effectiveness, and as a contrast to the sharp competitive edge required in the office. Educators use games for the same sorts of purposes, building group cohesion in the classroom, encouraging non-competitive play to enhance self-esteem, and encouraging creativity and lateral thinking. Through these improvements, games can promote achievement and empower learners.

Immodestly, I'd like to point to the gratifying success of Gamesters Handbooks' One and Two. Gamesters' One was published in England in 1978, and by 1991 it had arrived in Australia before I did. I successfully sold it in America when I was there myself in the 1980s. Over two hundred thousand copies have been sold to educators, social workers, management consultants, trainers, prison wardens, scout leaders, psychologists; in short, anyone who works with groups of any age or description.

The purpose of writing this book is not just to replicate the success of the first two. The only drawback to that success has been that because the books are sold alongside others in bookshops or at conferences, or borrowed from libraries, they are often used by people without any background or training in working with groups.

Sometimes it has been difficult for us to see meaningful games played meaninglessly or even damagingly, by people who don't understand their purpose or appreciate their potential. But that is a negative thought. To put it positively, the real aim of this book is to bring new games to the group worker's repertoire, but this time accompanied by commentary which will offer full understanding of their purpose, and their possible outcomes.

With John Norris

While making a return visit to England In June, 1977, on a Student-Centred Learning training day in a big college, I met up with John Norris. He remembered me from ten years earlier when I had led a similar staff development day at his school. I only vaguely remembered him, since it had been a very large group and a decade previously. But recognition dawned as soon as I realised that John is a Gamester like me, who sees the intrinsic value of non-competitive group games in teaching and training, and can invent new ones at a moment's notice. This chance meeting resulted in a delightful collaboration via technology that miraculously bridged the geographical distance between us. So throughout this book, when the word 'we' is used, it means Donna and John.

The Context

All of the games we present here are set in a context of Student-Centred Learning (SCL). For more detailed information about this philosophy and the methods it embodies, read *A Guide to Student-Centred Learning,* Brandes & Ginnis, 1986, Stanley Thornes (Publishers) Ltd.

SCL is a systematic approach to learning at any age and in any setting, in which the leader and participants are in partnership for the planning, organising and evaluating of all work and all business or projects. SCL has always been around, it is not new.

We know that there have always been teachers, including some of history's great ones like John Dewey, Carl Rogers, Sylvia Ashton Warner, and others as far back as Socrates, who believed that people learn best when they are:

a) discovering things for themselves, not being lectured or instructed;
b) enjoying themselves;
c) feeling in charge of themselves;
d) taking responsibility and ownership for their own learning.

In 1992, when the Regional Association for Student-Centred Learning was founded, we had as our Mission Statement, 'SCL: Mainstream by the Year 2000'.

This goal has been pursued and, in some aspects, achieved; many businesses and schools have taken on the philosophy and the methods, or have established long term plans to do so. There are many reasons for this change. People are realising that there is just too much information available now for us to think we can 'cover' a set curriculum. In Australia a group of industrialists met and formulated the Seven Key Competencies, which are summarised below. They indicate the kinds of skills that every student must master in order to be competent at work and in their daily lives. We believe that these could be the basis for a truly effective curriculum.

Seven Key Competences

For effective participation in the emerging patterns of work and work organisation

Collecting Analysing and Organising Information

The capacity to locate information, sift and sort information in order to select what is required and present it in a useful way, and evaluate both the information itself and the source and methods used to obtain it

Communicating Ideas and Information

The capacity to communicate effectively with others using the range of spoken, written, graphic and other non-verbal means of expression

Planning and Organising Activities
The capacity to plan and organise one's own work activities, including making good use of time and resources, sorting out priorities and monitoring one's own performance

Working with Others and in Teams
The capacity to interact effectively with other people both on a one-to-one basis and in groups, including understanding and responding to the needs of a client and working effectively as a member of a team to achieve a shared goal

Using Mathematical Ideas and Techniques
The capacity to use mathematical ideas, such as number and space, and techniques such as estimation and approximation, for practical purposes

Solving Problems
The capacity to apply problem solving strategies in purposeful ways, both in situations where the problem and the desired solution are clearly evident and in situations requiring critical thinking and a creative approach to achieve an outcome

Using Technology
The capacity to apply technology, combining the physical and sensory skills needed to operate equipment with the understanding of scientific and technological principals needed to explore and adapt systems

Another reason for the necessity of change is that we can no longer prepare people for specific jobs. The occupations that our students will pursue ten years from now have, in many cases, not even been invented yet.

Futurologists tell us that people will be moving around geographically and professionally, so that a person might have several different professions, not just jobs, in a lifetime. So preparation for adulthood must now include a set of skills, including numeracy and literacy, technological expertise, and the ability to cooperate, collaborate, and work independently.

Though science fiction sometimes depicts the worker of the future as a mindless drone, perhaps with a number instead of a name, we firmly believe that, on the contrary, employers will be continuing to want people who can think for themselves, see themselves as part of the whole picture at work, be effective problem-solvers and good team players. Organisations with this sort of attitude will benefit in terms of productivity as well as in worker/student satisfaction.

We notice that in an attempt to quantify productivity in our schools in the late 90s, there has grown to be an emphasis on 'accountability' – on measuring and monitoring, and publicly reporting outcomes. However, we believe this actually slows down and decreases achievement. We can have at our fingertips, given the resources, the technology to accurately record students' progress, and in fact the students can do most of this themselves in conjunction with the teacher. We do not need continual testing or publication of league tables, or competition between schools, to improve the quality of learning. We need upgrading and updating of teacher training, and resources within schools.

We believe that the activities in this book, if used purposefully, can go a long way to create a positive learning environment, within which effective learning is both increased and enjoyed by everyone involved. In doing this we can promote achievement and enhance the self-esteem, and therefore the learning potential, of every student.

Donna Brandes, with John Norris, October, 1997

Chapter One

Rationale, Guidelines and Ideas

Some General Guidelines for Gamesters

"A good leader not only knows how to teach games, but understands what each game has to offer to the group and to the individual participants – in addition to the sheer fun of playing."

Frank Harris[1]

Good games are full of learning and meaning. To ignore this fact and play only for fun is perfectly legitimate, of course, and is at the discretion of the leader and participants. But what we are advocating in this book is the use of games for personal, group, and organisational growth. For schools, in particular, we advocate the use of games to create a positive learning environment. Therefore, we would insist that careful choice, implementation, and evaluation or debriefing of games, is absolutely necessary for effective outcomes.

Perhaps this might seem obvious to the reader, but not to us. Based on experience and observation in hundreds of classrooms, and numerous organisations, we can say that many leaders pay attention to play, and not to process or effective outcome. So, at this point we need to talk about ways in which to play games thoughtfully and purposefully, so that the outcomes are noticeable and can be evaluated.

Choice of Game

Choosing the right game for the right moment is an art, and participants can become as skilled at it as the leaders. This avoids one of the dangers of the leader always choosing, which is that it can become very manipulative. A boss may decide to choose a game which will encourage the participants to confide in each other; if their intentions are not honourable, and agreements about confidentiality are not made and observed, then this is outright manipulation, which can be very harmful, and is to be avoided at all costs.

A teacher may think, 'My class is unsettled, I'll choose a game to calm them down' or, conversely, 'My class is lethargic, I'll choose a game to liven them up'. But, do we have the right to be in the business of mood control? It's a tricky question. In all honesty, we want the group to be functioning well, and a game that might facilitate this is perfectly justifiable.

We find that the best way to avoid manipulation is to be open about what we're doing. The opposite of manipulation is clear and direct communication. Manipulation is mostly underhanded, taking place without the knowledge and consent of the manipulatee, and with most of the benefits being for the manipulator. So as teachers, we could say something like, "It seems a bit wild in here. Any ideas about what we could do to settle down?" Then we are living our student-centred philosophy, and being true to the principles of consultation. Pupils may surprise you, and choose a few minutes of silent rest or meditation, if that has been introduced. They might choose to discuss in the group whatever they are feeling tense about. Or they may pick an appropriate game. And of course, we can participate in the choice as well, ruling out activities which will increase the commotion. Some games, like **How do you Like Your Neighbour? [p.56]** have a double-edged effect, and can be used for both calming down and livening up. The kids will realise this, because the games will have been debriefed after playing.

When you are embarking on a new topic, you can choose a game which will get the students thinking about what is to come. For instance, if you were about to study plants, you could suggest a game like **Name Six [p.27]**, where students would have to name various types of plants that they know something about already, such as "Name six kinds of citrus tree".

If the class is starting on a project, you could introduce one of the 'Big Games' **[see chapter 2]**, like **Territories [p.6]**, and continue the game from time to time where appropriate to the project.

Choosing a game like **Guess Who Said It [see Gamesters' Handbook S9]**, can be done quite deliberately, with the intention of building self-esteem and group trust, but then the game must be introduced and debriefed properly, in order to avoid manipulation.

Once a group has built up a repertoire of games, a choice can be offered to them, and they can learn to search for new games and to invent them for a specific purpose.

When do the Players Play?
a) The easy answer: Whenever you/we/they feel like it!
However, most teachers and leaders will tell you that this is not as easy as it seems. Their main criticism of games is invariably, "We don't have time for them, we have to cover the curriculum". But it's our contention that, on the contrary, if you build purposeful games into the curriculum, they will save you time in the long run. Sometimes teachers feel they have to settle for playing a game when there's a moment of spare time in the day. This of course is the most common usage of casual games. Ten minutes left? Let's have a round of **The Adverb Game [see Gamesters' Handbook C62]**, or, if the group is in a circle, **How Do You Like Your Neighbour?** This puts an enjoyable high spot into the day, and perhaps not much more. However, there will almost certainly be no time left for debriefing, which violates the 'always debrief' rule, mentioned in the next section. So to squeeze the most benefit out of your games, we recommend that this timing shouldn't happen too often.

b) Re-entry

Often a game at the beginning of a session, as soon as the group comes in, will deal with whatever baggage they bring in with them, help them past the wanting to chat stage, bring the members closer together, and prepare them for collaborative participative learning. A **Round [p.16]** is one of our favourite ways of starting a lesson, so in our classrooms we usually start with the chairs in a circle, or a comfortable place to sit down together. We expect that if we come in a bit late, the students will already be in the circle or on the rug, waiting and talking quietly. We will have practiced this behaviour many times, if necessary. If the group is in the middle of a project, a really good way to start is with a round of 'How far I've come, and where I'm going next' – not every day, but once in every few meetings.

c) Wrapping up a session

We like to have closure at the end of a meeting to find out what people thought about it, check on progress, or end on an active note. We'd suggest that it is worthwhile allowing time in your planning for a round or a short discussion, because it will increase continuity and sense of consultation.

d) To work on self-esteem

There are a number of activities in this book which are specifically aimed at enhancing self-esteem. But the very act of sitting down together, focussing and listening to each other, making a set of agreements to work by, and thus promoting a collaborative positive learning environment, goes a long way towards enhancing intrinsic self-confidence and sense of security. The way that problems are solved in the group enables students to feel, 'I can handle anything that comes along because I've learned the skills for listening and negotiating'.

e) For pastoral care

Many teachers don't choose to be part of a pastoral care or home-room program. They might think this is a waste of time, or argue "I'm getting paid to be a teacher, not a therapist". But we would argue that one of the things we must teach is social skills. If the school has a pastoral care system which involves being with the same group of students for a short period each day, the time could be well used in introducing some learning games so that the meeting is not just chat time, but is productive in terms of enhancing relationships and behaviour.

f) To introduce a new topic

For example, imagine the set curriculum requires us to teach a unit on Victorian England. Good practice demands that we investigate the prior knowledge of the students, and enable them to explore the topic freely, before settling down to specific learning. So, we might ask the students what they would expect to learn in a unit about England. We could brainstorm the answers. We could then ask them what problems they might encounter when exploring the topic, and engage in some problem-solving activities with them.

We could do a round to find out what especially interests each student, and then use that information to decide who is working alone, in pairs, or in groups, to research their specific information. Someone, student or teacher, could find out about Victorian games (for example), and lead the class in playing them.

g) When the students want to lead an activity
Students can invent new games and lead the class in trying them out, then record them for future use. Students can also choose games appropriate for current learning.

h) At staff meetings for team-building or problem-solving
An inspiring leader can introduce games for all of the reasons above, and can promote staff collegiality and productivity. A warm-up or a closing game is no more a waste of valuable time in the staff room than in the classroom; they can have the same positive team-building effects, and go a long way towards erasing some of the negative staff room behaviours like sarcasm, cliques, lack of respect for each other and gossip about pupils. The use of specific relevant activities can create a positive working environment which will break old patterns and set up newly productive ones.

i) When the game is the lesson
Some of the 'Big Games' can be used as lessons in themselves, to lead into project work. An example would be **Territories**.

TERRITORIES

AIMS:	Clarification of values, self-validation, group and social development.
MATERIALS:	Chairs and tables.
PROCEDURE:	1. Discuss how the world is broken up into different countries or states, and how each state makes its own laws within its boundaries.

6

2. Each individual marks out a territory, using chairs, tables, etc, and makes their own laws.
3. The leader tells everyone they are now free to move around, trade or enlarge their territories.

VARIATIONS: One individual could become the authority in a particular state and the others must follow their orders. Use real countries. Use real problems, e.g. lack of water, impending invasion.

TERRITORIES UNPACKED

When all of the stages have been carried out, the concept of designing a territory, state, or country from scratch can be discussed in depth. People could research, for instance, the concept of Government as we know it today originating in England, or the Declaration of Independence and the Constitution in the United States of America. Questions of immigration, like "Who do we allow or not allow into our Country?" will doubtless have come up during the game anyway, priming the students to consider those issues more seriously.

Debriefing and Questioning

Debriefing and questioning is where we discover whether an activity has been worthwhile, and for this reason should never be omitted unless absolutely necessary. We like to avoid telling participants at the beginning what an activity is going to be about, leaving them free to draw their own conclusions (as discussed earlier, an exception to this is when the choice of game could be construed as manipulative, in which case the motives behind the choice are laid bare to the participants before the game is started). So it is particularly important to remember to ask participants at the end of the game what they learned, what they noticed, and what they will be taking away with them from the experience.

If we do not debrief or question at the end of an activity, we have the phenomenon of what we call an 'empty' game – devoid of meaning or lasting effect. Participants in any group activity must be given time to reflect. The skilled use of questioning provides several effective outcomes:

  a) the reflection is carried out for the benefit of everyone concerned;
  b) closure is reached;
  c) evaluation is accomplished and its results noted for the future;
  d) people go away having felt a sense of purpose to what they were doing.

Sometimes students quip "We've just been playing, when do we start working?" So we need to discuss the concept of the difference between work and play, and also reinforce the idea that we can be working in school without being seen to be writing. The dictionary defines play as 'exercise or action by way of amusement or recreation', and work as, 'effort directed to produce or accomplish something'. So we can see that if we don't reflect on learning, and don't make sure that the students see the purpose in what they've accomplished, we are setting them up for a conversation at home which goes:

Parent   What did you learn today?
Kid   Nothing, in maths we just played games.

This conversation is a good recipe for bringing parents rushing to your classroom in varying degrees of high dudgeon, demanding to know why you're wasting their children's time.

Of course we don't want that, but more important for the intrinsic learning of the students, is that they feel a sense of purpose and understand the relevance of every single thing they do in school. It doesn't matter whether we debrief with discussion, with a round, or with some journal writing followed by short discussion, as long as the reflection stage is not missed out.

So we leave this discussion with three key words: DEBRIEF! DEBRIEF! DEBRIEF!

The Role of Games in Organisations

" … encouraging worker participation in management is like letting monkeys out of the zoo."

A manager's comment, from Skynner and Cleese[2]

In this chapter we have drawn a parallel between organisations in industry, public service, and the education system. We won't go into an analysis of similarities and differences between these environments, but we will look at some of the changes that have been taking place in all sorts of large organisations, including schools. One of the texts we have used is by Skynner and Cleese, so we acknowledge them while filtering their material through our own backgrounds in many different organisations, including educational settings, so that we have synthesised our experience with theirs.

It is our contention that people achieve most in environments where risks, mistakes, and even failure, as well as success, are seen as productive factors in organisational growth. We are impressed by the notion that a successful organisation is one 'where people can fail safely'. In fact, we would go as far as saying that once you are failing safely, you are actually not failing at all. Without an

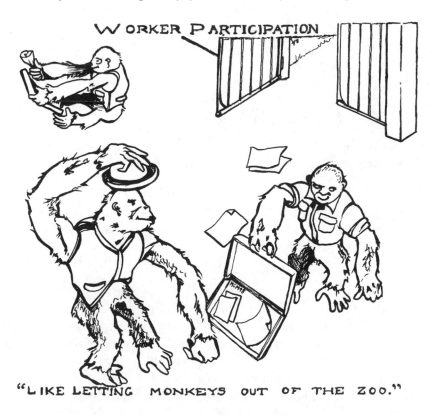

WORKER PARTICIPATION

"LIKE LETTING MONKEYS OUT OF THE ZOO."

acceptance that life's endeavours don't always run smoothly, that we must all fail sometimes in order to learn and grow, it is more likely that members of a team become reluctant to take risks, thus blocking personal, professional, and institutional growth.

During the 1980s many organisations within industry, commerce and the public sector, began to recognise the need for flatter management structures to encourage effective and productive networks. Such recognition often included systems of quality control (carried out by representatives from all levels of an organisation), target-setting, developmental planning, appraisal and the recording of achievement. This movement was, and is, reflected in school systems, where all of the above processes have been recommended, and in some cases implemented.

However, all of these processes depend on trust, and in many cases the importance of that issue isn't addressed. Most organisations could, if they looked closely, detect hidden messages of trust and mistrust within their management structure and interpersonal relationships. For example, a public relations company may suffer from its inability to recognise gender issues within its line management system. So could a school. Schools may neglect to tackle, seriously, issues of sarcasm, teasing or bullying in the classroom, playground, and especially the staff room, where sarcasm is purportedly seen as harmless, friendly banter, when in fact the staff room is the wellspring of the ethos of the school. Likewise, business organisations can be undermined around the coffee machine or water-cooler, where gossip and rumours float around along with the liquids imbibed. This can be seen to happen even where there is an official rhetorical emphasis on the personal development, confidence, and self-esteem of the employees or students, and even when an organisation claims, "We care about our employees!" "We put our students first!"

We believe that such hidden issues stifle personal creativity and sense of responsibility, providing barriers to organisational growth.

Then there is the question of employee or student participation in management. Ideas about good leadership have changed radically in the last few decades. Old–style leadership rests on the assumption that 'the boss knows best'. So, naturally, all the other people in the organisation are treated like an inferior species. The boss uses only a limited range of each employee's talents and skills, and consequently is often not interested in any of their other abilities.

The advantage of this style was that the boss maintained complete control, and could make autocratic decisions, without the laborious process of consultation. This style costs less in terms of time and money, but only initially. The disadvantages were many, and often ignored at the risk of productivity and worker/student satisfaction. The boss might be given inaccurate information, since negative feedback would be filtered out. New ideas did not circulate freely.

Implementation of orders was carried out by people who did not understand the thinking behind them. Fear would be the motivation for workers/students, which often caused them to behave cautiously and defensively.

New–style management makes a different basic assumption, namely that: The people closest to the work know best about productivity.

Some of the implications of this are:

- people are treated holistically, as complete human beings;
- all of the workers' knowledge, talents and skills are available to the organisation;
- emotional needs are taken into account;
- people tend to be more motivated and contribute and achieve more;
- leaders have a much wider and more encompassing view of how people are performing, and can make more informed decisions;
- everyone is involved in the assessment and evaluation processes;
- control, and thus responsibility, is spread throughout the system;
- the management structure flattens, so that the organisation provides fertile ground for developing new leaders.

We believe and indeed intend that this book promotes activities designed to achieve the above objectives.

If an organisation decides to address these issues actively, they may turn to the use of consultants who are specialised in building synergy and trust. In the past few decades we have seen the increasing popularity of setting up with consultants, programmes of outdoor pursuits, providing personal and team challenges designed to promote trust and self-confidence. Such ideas have proliferated throughout the western world. Often activities such as abseiling, wilderness trekking, survival activities, and crossing vast gorges on ropes, are part of a company's or school's development program.

Individuals and teams frequently make tremendous strides while away, involved in outdoor pursuits, with people coming back relaxed, refreshed, feeling good about themselves and each other. Of course, these exercises must take place out of the usual work setting, which is both an advantage in terms of the absence of work distractions and patterns which offers the possibility for complete refreshment, and a drawback in terms of time and money.

The beauty of most of the activities in this book is that they require little preparation, almost no cost, and can be engaged in whenever and wherever appropriate. Most of them are non-competitive, so that personal growth is facilitated within each individual.

Issues of trust can be addressed both deliberately and incidentally through the activities in this book, and we believe that this applies to any group, from schools, through all sorts of training groups in community services, to major industrial organisations. Certain basic activities such as brainstorming, problem-solving, clarification of values and role-play, can help to release the creative potential of any group, and thus facilitate achievement. A supportive and non-threatening environment, we believe, can uphold greater involvement in organisational decision-making and target-setting.

What is a Positive Learning Environment?

"The mission of the schools is to teach children no matter what their state of readiness. When traditional and conventional practices do not succeed, the school is responsible for finding other means of teaching effectively and, if necessary, for changing its concepts and methods drastically in order to do so."

Weinstein and Fantini[3]

The concept of a Positive Learning Environment (PLE) is applicable to any organisation. To make the writing and reading here less unwieldy, we are setting these ideas in a context of schools. However, businesses and industries also reflect the recent emphasis on being a Learning Company, because they know that where people are engaged in lifelong learning they are more alive and more productive. Thus, all of the ideas below can be transferred to any work setting, including the staff room, and even to families as well. Games can go a long way towards developing this lively and enthusiastic atmosphere, especially if they are group-building games and not highly competitive.

Safety in the classroom

The classroom environment is probably the most important aspect of effective teaching. For students to be able to learn, they need to feel safe and responsible for their own learning. Safety is the prime consideration. Though most teachers take good care for physical safety, and show a lot of concern for running, falling, tripping over each other, leaning back in chairs, using lab and kitchen equipment, etc, unfortunately many of our classrooms are emotionally unsafe.

Students can be seen to be afraid to speak out about their ideas and opinions. They are often shy in front of their peers, fearing ridicule or unpopularity. Kids who are too bright tend to be put down, and kids who are slower are the butt of other students' jokes and nicknames. So in a lot of classes we can notice that students walk a fine line of mediocrity, trying to please their peers and their teachers, afraid to be themselves.

In an emotionally safe classroom, it is fun to bounce around new ideas, knock them down, build them up and invent new ones. Everyone can contribute and work at their own pace. Kids aren't afraid to say, respectfully, what they think and feel. People don't sabotage or sneer at each other's work. Problems can be shared and resolved by the group. Consultation among the partners–in–learning happens as a matter of course in all aspects of group life. New people can enter the room and be welcomed and accepted, proactively, by the group.

Mistakes

In a classroom where the atmosphere is positive, the students and teacher can make mistakes and learn from them. Mistakes are valued because they indicate that people have felt safe enough to take risks. Mistakes can sometimes indicate carelessness or inaccuracy, but they can also show that people have been using scientific method, hazarding guesses and formulating hypotheses.

In a student-centred classroom, these sorts of mistakes are valued and encouraged and do not receive a mocking or scolding response. Instead, there is always encouragement to check the accuracy of a statement or an outcome.

To illustrate the difference between a didactic and a student-centred response to mistakes, take this example from a primary classroom:

Teacher   We are going to visit a farm next week. What animals do you think we will find?

[*Students offer many answers such as 'cows', 'horses', 'pigs', 'deer', 'budgies', 'sheep', 'goats', 'elephants'.*]

Teacher   Yes, most of those are right. We would find sheep, cows, horses, pigs, deer and goats. We probably wouldn't find a budgie on a farm, unless it was a pet inside the house, or in an aviary outside. We wouldn't find an elephant, because they are not a farm animal. Remember, a farm is there so people can raise animals and crops to give us food to live on.

That might be the usual sort of conversation with a more traditional, didactic teacher. The teacher feels it is important to only have the correct answers and implies that s/he is the only source of the correct information.

Another sort of response from an SCL teacher might be:

Teacher   OK. We have produced a good list there. I'll make sure everyone gets a copy to take with them to the farm next week. We will be able to check the animals off as we see them. So, why do we have farms anyway? What do you think they are for? Let's talk about their purposes. We could see what we notice when we go there.

It is important to point out that the SCL teacher is not encouraging false information or inaccuracies, what they have done, deliberately, is to adopt a 'wait and see' attitude, in order to train the students to hypothesise, observe and check their own ideas for correctness. The underlying purpose is to spark their curiosity and deepen their understanding.

So you can see that the whole concept of a mistake has been changed from being something born of stupidity or misinformation, to being seen as a crucial learning experience. In order for a conversation like the one above to take place, two concepts need to replace traditional thinking:

a) the teacher has to relinquish being the only source of correct and relevant information so that the students can learn experientially;

b) the students will have to be told initially, and then become accustomed to having a much more open approach. They will have to learn to stop ridiculing people who take risks and make mistakes.

It is conceded that this type of conversation takes a lot more time. Even the most dedicated SCL teachers may not always choose under pressure to allow this much open discussion. But this should be the usual approach to new information because the time spent will be made up by greater retention and deeper comprehension.

Diversity

In an SCL classroom, or organisation, people value each other's diversity. Therefore, no one is ridiculed or insulted. Each person in the classroom can develop and share their skills. Gender and colour issues are dealt with in the group, and an attempt is made to redress imbalances for each child's learning style and skills.

Pace and Style

People can learn at their own pace, and in their own style. There is no pressure to be achieving at a 'group rate' where some students may be held back and others are pushed too hard.

Attention is paid to various learning styles, so that teaching methods must be consistently changing from visual to audial, from kinesthetic to interpersonal.

People are equally skilled at working independently and collaboratively. Students can work alone, in pairs, in small groups and in the whole group, so that they are skilled in every combination.

Assessment

Students are skilled at evaluating themselves and their peers realistically, giving suggestions for changes and improvements alongside positive feedback for their work. They can be trained to do this, so that they are capable of setting criteria and goals, using checksheets on student outcomes, deciding what needs to be amended or expanded, and consulting with the teacher about grades and marks when necessary. Grades and marks are kept to a minimum, with portfolios of selected work representing accountability.

[By the way, this is partly for the benefit of the teachers, who should not be staggering home with piles of marking each night, but should be free to rest, relax, enjoy their families and their own personal health and fitness.]

Everyone has the right to learn and be productive. Learning is fun when there is no fear of failure and every day provides an experience of success.

Training for PLE

Students and staff alike may need to be trained to promote a PLE, and this will take time at first, but will save countless hours of struggle later on. This is where the use of non-competitive games can be extremely useful. The following are two examples of games designed to facilitate PLE.

Example I
THE ROUND

AIMS: To discuss solutions to a problem, to air feelings, to share knowledge, to make plans, to conduct evaluations. To provide a structured and calm way of encouraging pupils to speak to each other and the teacher. This is a time when everyone has an opportunity to speak, in turn, without being forced to do so. To encourage participation by removing the fear of being ridiculed or ignored; everyone is guaranteed a hearing. To acknowledge that everyone has an equally valid and valuable contribution to make. Thereby, to contribute towards raising self-esteem.

MATERIALS: None.

PROCEDURE:
1. Everyone sits in a circle.
2. The leader explains the 'rules': Anyone may start by saying something, then each person will have a chance to speak in turn around the circle. No one may comment, verbally or non-verbally, negatively or positively on what anyone says. No one may interrupt. Anyone can say 'pass' when it is their turn.
3. The leader explains that the spirit of the round is that it affords an opportunity for everybody to listen to each other. Discussion can come later.
4. Someone begins.

VARIATIONS: Paper Round. This variation is especially useful when class members are not confident enough to express personal opinions in public. The Paper Round can be seen as a step towards a full round. Give everyone a piece of paper and a pencil. Ask for contributions to be written individually and anonymously. Papers are folded, collected in a container and shaken. Pass the container round the circle, each person taking out one piece of paper. Individuals take turns to read the papers, each reading the anonymous comment as if it were their own. This can be a helpful way of handling sensitive material.

SOURCE: Paul Ginnis

Example II
THE RULE OF THE GAME

AIMS:	Group interaction, imagination, intellectual exercise, fun, getting to know each other.
MATERIALS:	None.
PROCEDURE:	1. Everyone sits in a circle.
	2. One person goes out. The others choose a rule. When the person comes back in (after a set time) they must attempt to discover what the rule is by asking the others questions about themselves, simple ones that the Questioner can SEE the answers to, like "What colour are your socks?" In this way the Questioner can observe and find out what the rule is. A good rule to begin with is to answer every question as if you were the person sitting on your right. Players must answer questions honestly and consistently, according to the rules they have agreed on. Another example of a good rule is for all the women to tell lies and all the men tell the truth.
VARIATIONS:	Rules can be complex or very simple, according to age and experience. Rules can be visual, e.g. scratch head before answering, or structural, e.g. each answer begins with the next letter of the alphabet.

THE RULE OF THE GAME UNPACKED

Since this game was first published in Gamesters' One, it has grown and changed enormously with very frequent usage. There are many similar games in the world's gamelore, such as **Crossed and Uncrossed**, where the rule is that you cross your legs before you answer, or suchlike. But the reasons why it is a seminal game are that it has many distinct benefits, unequalled by any other game we know of:

a) it is totally portable, can be played in a car, bus, pub, auditorium with hundreds of people, at parties, or most especially in the classroom;

b) it is completely flexible as to who can play it; old or young, gamesters or not, I have never known a group that did not respond;

c) it is the response that it elicits from participants that makes it so valuable. Within the first two or three turns of playing, the group invariably starts to support the person who goes out. Everyone can feel that change happening; everyone starts to help, to encourage, to give hints, sometimes even going so far that they give the game away. So, in this sense, it is a superb tool for building a safe and supportive learning environment;

d) it is completely adaptable to learning uses, in that all subjects, and all enterprises, have patterns to them which can be discovered, applied and then
   transferred to other subjects; **[see the interview with Tony Harris, p.26]**

e) even if you ask kids what they've learnt by playing this, they can always tell
   you accurately the points above, which does not always happen in other
   games;

f) not least of all, it is such fun, and I can remember playing at a Rotary Club
   meeting, with some very sceptical rural farmers. Within ten minutes, they
   were laughing and coming up with ideas, and when I asked them what they
   thought the game had to do with learning, they could easily make all of the
   points above, and more of their own. Next to charades, this has always been
   my very favourite game, and it has the advantage which charades does not,
   of needing absolutely no previous organisation or planning. You can get it
   together on the spur of the moment, and then use it afterwards to promote
   lateral thinking, discovery, and self-confidence, and most importantly, positive group feelings.

The Import/Export Model

The teacher teaches the students to learn. This simple proposition rests on many
theoretical and implied assumptions:

- that the authority of the teacher rests on his/her 'expert' status, supported
  by the successful completion of several 'rites of passage', examination successes, certificates, qualifications, university degrees, etc;
- that the learner is, in effect, an 'empty vessel', to be 'filled up' with the
  knowledge possessed by the teacher;
- that the learner brings little of significant value to the educational process;
- that experience is, at best, a rather second rate form of knowledge, essentially lacking validity and inherently subjective;
- that 'knowledge' is somehow, objective, and that the art of teaching lies in
  the transmission of this knowledge;
- that thought is an intrinsically higher form of knowledge than feeling.

The 'Hidden Curriculum' of Questioning

Questions, it may be contended, are an effective tool, in ensuring that what is
taught, is also learnt. We believe, however, that questioning is a complex process
of social interaction, often related to hidden agendas of power, authority, status,
ownership and control. We believe that effective questioning has an emotional
agenda, relating to issues of empowerment, creativity, discovery, autonomy and
trust.

Questioning

In the form of a Paper Round John asked a group of fourteen year olds to write down their feelings on 'Good' and 'Bad' questions used by teachers and adults. Here is what they said:

Good Questions ...

... are asked nicely,
are approached sensitively,
have more than one answer,
don't have one word answers,
may be repeated,
are explained,
make you think,
are not harmful,
are understandable,
are clear,
are confidently asked,
are productive,
get you thinking,
get to the point,
give you time to think,
don't leave people out,
are not too long,
are interesting,
are sometimes funny,
make you feel happy,
have feeling behind them,
are spoken in a nice tone,
make sense,
can be added to,
make more questions,
get your attention,
are well answered,
can be hard.

Bad Questions ...

... are badly answered,
are sarcastic,
try to put you down,
offend,
are not relevant,
are shouted,
make no sense,
are too long,
have no need to be asked,
have no variety of answers,
put you in a difficult position,
have one word answers,
are rude,
are too personal,
are too quick,
are unexpected,
are harmful to others,
are impossible to answer,
are not clear.

Questioning Unpacked

We analyse below, a series of questions, which might be commonly used in classroom situations. Our endeavour is to 'unpack' the implicit (or perhaps explicit!) messages which they contain.

1. **Q.** "What evidence can you present to support that statement?"

   Messages: You are confusing opinion with fact.

   This environment is an academic arena, evidence is your passport to admission.

   I know the evidence, perhaps you do not.

   I do not like what you are saying.

2. **Q.** "How can you possibly say that?"

   Messages: I do not value what you have to say.

   I think that your opinions are stupid.

   I am the judge of what is valid.

3. **Q.** "I am sure that we would all benefit from your wisdom, so please tell us more."

   Messages: My syntax is superior to yours.

   I will use sarcasm to demonstrate my superiority.

   I am in control.

4. **Q.** "What, I think you are trying to say is … "

   Messages: You cannot express yourself effectively.

   I will have to express your opinions for you.

   I have the power to do that.

5. **Q.** "Do not tell me what you feel, tell me what you think."

   Messages: My intellect is superior to your emotions.

   Your feelings count for little.

6. **Q.** "Can you help me understand that point a little more?"

   Messages: You own the point.

   I need you to help me if I am to understand it fully.

   We are both empowered.

7. **Q.** "How could we find out the answer to that question?"

   Messages: I am not the fount of knowledge.

   Alternative ways of finding the answer exist.

   The question belongs to all of us.

8. **Q.** "Is there anybody who disagrees with that?"

   Messages: It is OK to disagree.

   There does not need to be complete agreement.

   It is OK to challenge.

9. **Q.** "When is it OK to lie?"

   Messages: There may not be an absolute moral code.

   This is an open issue.

   I have not prejudged the outcome.

   We own the question.

10. **Q.** "How do you feel about that?"

    Messages: You own your feelings.

    Your emotional response is valuable.

    You are important.

We are not criticising the use of different types of questions for different purposes. Clearly, questions can be used to test factual recall, knowledge and understanding, conceptual awareness and the ability to synthesise and evaluate.

However, we are promoting the view that feeling and thinking are closely related processes, and that good questioning recognises this. Rather than the Import/Export model we would argue for emotional equality in the classroom, work place and conference centre. Our aim is to elicit good answers from good questions, and hence to ensure greater understanding of personal development.

Our experiences of working with people, tell us that 'unpacking' the hidden emotional agendas of individuals and groups (Will I be laughed at? Can I trust you? What if I'm wrong? What about my feelings of worthlessness? Will I be embarrassed?) is an essential pre-requisite to effective questioning, and therefore, effective learning. Many of the activities in this book, are designed to help group leaders with the process of 'unpacking'.

Student-Centred Learning Philosophy

"I have just realised that if I just start using one strategy after another, they will not work as well as if I really take on some changes in my attitudes and ways of working, even deeply understand the philosophy of Student-Centred Learning . . ."

Anonymous

The philosophy of student-centred learning is based on the humanistic psychology of Carl Rogers. Rogers has outlined the following basic outcomes of a student-centred approach:[4]

The Student . . .

- will feel more free to express both positive and negative feelings in class – towards other students, the teacher and content material;
- will tend to work through these feelings towards a realistic relationship, instead of burying them until they are explosive;
- will have more energy to devote to learning, because they will have less fear of continual evaluation and punishment;
- will discover they have a responsibility for their own learning, as they become more of a participant in the group learning process;
- will feel free to take off on exciting avenues of learning, with more assurance that their teacher will understand;
- will find that both their awe of authority and their rebellion against authority diminish, as they discover teachers and administrators to be fallible human beings, relating in imperfect ways to students;
- will find that the learning process enables them to grapple directly and personally with the problem of the meaning of their lives.

Many teachers ask us for strategies for student-centred learning. We're happy to provide these. But without the philosophy, methods and skills, the strategies are empty, purposeless and often won't work to produce effective results. At the heart of the student-centred approach is self-assessment. The following (slightly paraphrased) are some general principles of assessment outlined by Stephen Munby.[5]

Assessment of Personal Performance

General Principles of Assessment

1. *There should be an emphasis on achievement rather than failure.*
2. *Assessment approaches should be accompanied by flexibility and sensitivity on the part of the teacher (or boss).*
3. *They should aim to help rather than hinder learning.*
4. *They should aim to improve communication and relationships between assessor and the person being assessed.*
5. *Materials used for assessment … should be 'user-friendly', that is, understandable and usable by students (or workers).*
6. *Assessment approaches should be feasible and manageable.*

Just as students and teachers ought to be checking on their own performance and their own progress towards their personal and learning goals, so members of any organisation can be encouraged to keep track of how they are doing at all times, so that there are no sudden surprises when a boss calls on a worker to report back.

Assessment can be terribly misused, and can be competitive where it could be collaborative. It can be very discouraging, when it could just as well be affirming and motivating. Leaders can reassure workers that assessment is for the purpose of enhancing personal development, and everyone in the company can keep working towards better performance and stronger self-esteem. Far from being threatening, the processes of assessment and evaluation ought to be satisfying, and even motivating for all concerned. Each person in an organisation should be knowledgeable about how their performance will be measured, and should feel at ease in the process.

The SWIB Assessment

Organisations have long used a format for performance measurement called SWOT, which stands for Strengths, Weaknesses, Opportunities and Threats. This is considered a very practical tool, because it can be used at all levels of an organisation. We have changed it to SWIB, for which the framework is shown below. We like the word Barriers better than Threats because Threat implies outside force, while Barriers can build up from within or without.

Strengths	Weaknesses
(e.g.) I am very creative	(e.g.) I am usually late
I will walk every day	I never feel like walking when I wake up
Intentions	Barriers

The SWIB document can be used at regular intervals, say quarterly or semesterly. It can be filled out alone, by the individual whose performance is being assessed, and then discussed in a supportive manner with a supervisor or a peer. We have used it with pairs of team members, who then talked it over in a threesome with the leader or teachers.

Being able to set goals, keep track of progress, and then realistically assess strengths and weaknesses, become aware of how barriers arise, and how to take advantage of opportunities for growth; all of these are signs of healthy learning, and are skills to be learned over a lifetime.

This is not the arena in which to analyse assessment and recording in depth. Instead, we just wanted to make the few points above.

Inventing New Games

Inventing new games can be a very amusing challenge for leaders, students and staff alike. Of course, don't invent too many, or people like us will go out of business. But sometimes it really is fun to let students see how far their creativity will stretch, and if you are the teacher or leader, you will never be short of new activities.

I suggest with students that you could play the game **Anarchy**. The instructions are simple. Ask your students to form groups of 5. Then ask them to invent, in silence, a game that has no rules.

What usually happens is that someone will start performing an action, say, jumping up and down. Someone else will follow, and immediately they have a rule, which is 'follow the leader'. There can't be any rules, so they have to start the game again. Often there is a degree of frustration while people go through the process of realising that unless everyone acts absolutely independently, they are going to end up with at least one rule. If people are acting individually, and idiosyncratically, then the result will be Anarchy. Defined in the dictionary as 'lawlessness and disorder'.

In the discussion that follows, people will get the idea that in a game, a set of rules are necessary, and that if they're not followed, chaos reigns, and the game loses its structure and excitement. For those creatures that teachers call 'difficult kids' who will often exploit or ignore the rules, this experience can be helpful.

I would then suggest playing **The Rule of the Game [p.17]**, which is unpacked earlier in this chapter. A discussion could follow about how rules are constructed, what they're for, and which kinds are needed or not needed for inventing new games.

In scL, though, another step might be necessary, in which you have a debate about non-competitive versus competitive games, and the group decides which they want to invent.

Now you're probably ready. Small groups could form, and could brainstorm topics for which new games would be useful. In putting this book together, John's classes, and other groups of kids, have invented lots of new games, so don't think that only adults can do this. After all, if you think about it, little kids invent new games by the dozen while they are absorbed in natural play. The only difference between that and the inventions in school, is that perhaps the school ones are going to be set up to achieve certain goals, besides just having fun.

I remember when I was in California, and teaching units on Mexico, how my students invented dramas and games, new ones each day, to fit the topic. We built an Aztec pyramid, which was a two dimensional stage set, propped against a wall, with steps leading up to it. We started off by holding a human sacrifice each day at 2pm. We manufactured blood, and swords, and the deaths became increasingly gory, so that other classes begged to come in and watch. But even the bloodthirsty Year 6s tired of that, and they began to invent challenges by which intended victims could escape death. If they could climb the steps blind-folded and backwards without faltering, if they could outrun their captors on the field … if they could think of a way to outwit the Spanish Conquistadores … then they could earn a reprieve. I think we could have gone on forever.

On a more sophisticated level, perhaps you can think of a problem that arises in your staff meetings. You and an ally could invent a game that the staff could play which would highlight and solve that problem. If your family has arguments over chores, then ask your kids to invent a game that will decide arbitrarily who does what.

Remember, games are also based on a sense of fairness, on honour, and on integrity, otherwise they are no fun. So inventing purpose-built games can be a way of instilling those particular virtues, without punishment or sermonising.

Best of all, perhaps, this is something you can try tomorrow in your classroom or staff room. Take the topic at hand, say fractions. Ask the students to invent a game that illustrates exactly how to add fractions. They can use paper, people, pies, or whatever they want as materials.

Let's say a major problem in the school revolves around the rigidity of timetabling. Spend some meeting time, a limited amount, asking the staff to play with ideas for increasing flexibility of timing throughout the school, to make space for team-teaching and for appropriate regroupings when needed. You may be astonished at some of the ideas that come up, especially if you are the person who has been using the same grid system all along.

If your organisation lacks a sense of synergy, brainstorming for games which would increase the power and productivity of the team could be fun in itself, and could provide an opportunity to implement newly created ideas, which will compound the feeling of working together as equal partners.

So, while we invite you to own and treasure the games we've provided, we also challenge you to see what you can produce for yourselves.

Case Studies of SCL in Action

Interview with Tony Harris

Tony Harris is Head of English at Belmont Senior High School, one of the two schools in Western Australia that have taken on student-centred learning as a specific, systematic, whole school approach. Tony has been one of the prime movers in this process, having been the one who found me in the first place, and arranged to have me in to work with the staff.

The Principal of Belmont has been wholly supportive and enthusiastic about SCL as well, which is another reason why the initiative has been so successful.

Tony is my closest educational colleague in Australia, and I know from teaching with him every year since 1991 that he is intrinsically and wholeheartedly devoted to SCL as being the specific system of choice for the future. I also know that Tony uses games in the context of SCL, and does so with enjoyment and effectiveness. So, I asked him if he would like to talk about how he uses games in his work.

Tony's response:

"I use games for a wide variety of purposes. I use them to establish a positive learning environment, in the early stages with a new class, while we're becoming acquainted. I use them to teach cooperative and listening skills, and also for revision and creative thinking. I try not to use games to manipulate moods, or to settle a class down if they arrive feeling too hyper and exuberant. I don't use them that way because I feel they are too important and valuable to waste like that. I do have certain settling activities that I use, for example working on spelling. Kids have partners, and we choose their twenty words a week in a variety of ways, either from a standardised list, or from novels we're reading, or each partner chooses ten, and they swap lists and practice together. In any case, this seems to settle them and get them ready to work on literature, and also to establish routines and productive behaviours."

"But I see games as very important in other ways. Let's take **The Rule of the Game [p.17]**, for instance, which is one of my favourites. It is the game which I use most often, with the most people. It teaches listening, and almost always results in cooperative behaviours, as students begin to support the person facing the problem. It's also good for verbal skills and lateral thinking, and it engages everyone. So in lower school, I might take a page of words from a text, and circle some words. In groups, they would have to figure out why those particular words are circled – what the rule is."

"In Year 12 Literature, I might give them a list of characters from all the novels they've read, and they would have to discover what those characters have in

26

common, for example, male characters that have come to grief through the love of a woman."

"When there are 35 kids, the circle becomes too big, so we play in two groups. I wander back and forth, and if they lose focus, or if I don't agree with how they're going, I'll sit down with that group for a while and we'll discuss it."

"I use it with Year 10s just to establish patterns, and they will design lists, and then swap their lists with other groups to find the rules. They might be lists of numbers which might turn out to be their own phone numbers, or they'll list all the train stations on a certain route. They become more and more inventive. They made a list of animals which were more than animals, but also the names of football teams – a list within a list."

"Another favourite of mine is **Pig, Wolf and Farmer [p.58]**. It's just so much fun, but it also involves cooperation, teamwork, and strategic thinking. Paradoxically, it works better with older kids. Younger kids think it's too childish, and they get embarrassed if we play it outside where other students can see them squealing like pigs or growling and baring their claws. Older kids love to play it, and enjoy feeling childish again. Actually, we use it most successfully with adults in training sessions; they never seem to mind the opportunity to laugh a lot and be a bit foolish in this particular game."

"Another game which I use a lot for revision is **Name Six**."

NAME SIX

AIMS:	Concentration, quick thinking, fun, creativity, language development.
MATERIALS:	None.
PROCEDURE:	1. Group members sit in a circle with the person who is 'It' in the centre.
	2. The person who is 'It' closes his/her eyes.
	3. An object is passed quickly around the circle until 'It' says, "Stop".
	4. Whoever has the object is 'It 2'.
	5. 'It' gives 'It 2' a letter, such as P.
	6. The object is passed round the circle as quickly as possible and 'It 2' must think of six nouns that begin with P before the object comes back round to them.
	7. If he/she fails to do this, they go into the centre.
	8. Otherwise 'It' stays in the centre and the game starts again.

"In Year 12 Literature we use it to revise sections from the course, *Hamlet* for example. We might ask 'It' to name three characters that Hamlet most admires. Or, in *The Handmaid's Tale*, we might say, 'Name three colours that were associated with different women, and say what they signified, such as green for martyrs, red for breeders, white for purity'."

"Sometimes, if I think our 'people skills' need refreshing, we might play a number of games, briefly for seven to ten minutes each, in quick succession, like, two rounds of **The Rule of the Game**, three or four of **How Do You Like Your Neighbour [p.56]**, and two of **Name Six**, debriefing each one as we go. They refresh our skills and remind us of what we have agreed about how we will treat each other."

"We work in teaching teams with our Year 8s, so they have the same four teachers for almost all their subjects. We use the games during our Contact Time with those groups, and they will teach me a game they learned in another class, and *vice versa*. They love to teach the teachers, and the other classes, how to play a game. Even one boy we have who is particularly loud and obstructive, really enjoys teaching us a game we don't know."

"We make up quiz games a lot, and use them for revision, and for general knowledge. We also make up relays and use them to fit words and sentences and parts of speech together."

"In other words, I see games as useful learning tools, and use them regularly to enliven my classes, and encourage other teachers to do the same."

Interview with Sarah Carver

I chose to interview Sarah Carver because she is a young teacher (aged 25), with almost two years of teaching experience, and yet she is naturally student-centred in her approach to teaching and learning. Her students consistently create interesting and innovative projects, in partnership with Sarah, and she is careful to consult them at every stage of their process.

DB: Would you like to tell me how you use games in your work?

SC: I use them in lots of different ways. First of all, when I meet a new class, to break down barriers and build some trust. Then I like to link them into the subject areas, which for me are mostly Health and Social Studies. I also use them to introduce new topics.

DB: Could you give me some examples?

SC: Recently, my Year 8s were going to do a project on Families. So, I chose the game **Freud**, from Gamesters' Handbook Two, **[p.61]**. My plan was to use this to break into groups, and also to warm up, and link into families. At first they were very uncomfortable with it, because they weren't happy to sit on each other's knees at the end of each round. But they didn't want to give up, and I remembered what you said about keeping going when things got tough. So first we did it by standing in a line when we'd found our families, then by making a family statue as soon as we got together, and finally, they had a lot of fun sitting on each other.

DB Comment: *Some people would say they shouldn't be comfortable touching each other, but we think that healthy and easy ways of making contact are really good, breaking down gender barriers to friendship, and giving people a much higher degree of personal comfort.*

Sarah's given a perfect example here of not giving up just because things get uncomfortable or difficult. Those tricky points are where learning and growth can happen if we push past them. So she asked the students what to do, and they came up with a good progression.

SC: So, after we played the game pretty well, we stayed in the groups that came out of it, so we had groups of Mama, Papa, Young One, and Baby, and we brainstormed in those groups the roles of the different family members. We talked about expectations, and behaviour, and duties, and needs. We then blackboarded the results.

One of the kids raised the point that not all families were like this; they didn't all have two kids, two parents, a dog and a cat. So then we listed all the different kinds of families there could be. The interesting thing was that we decided at the end that all families still had similar kinds of needs, no matter who lived in them. I noticed that all the needs that were mentioned

29

were practical, to do with food and clothes, and planning things. No mention so far of love or nurturing, or the lack of it.

To get into the feelings aspect, we stayed in the groups and discussed and named ten things that most annoyed them about their families. From those suggestions, each group had to plan a short presentation, a song, a play, or a poem, whatever they wanted. One boy felt bad and worried about the negative view of family life that we were showing. I talked to him, and asked him what he wanted to do. He didn't want to work alone, and finally he decided just to observe.

DB: Did you then go on to show a more positive view of families?

SC: Yes, they went on to write a script about conflict and resolution. They came up with great scripts, and did some really good plays, costumes and all. We filmed the whole activity, and then played it back and evaluated it. Every kid was involved, even the one that had been sitting out.

DB: Sounds really good! I'd love to see the film … any other examples?

SC: With the Year 10s, getting ready for group work on projects. We used jigsaw puzzles of maps of the world, just on paper, with 20 pieces per table to make 4 maps. The rule was they had to be silent while they were doing it. Afterwards we talked about how they negotiated without talking, whether they were snatching and grabbing, whether they were meticulous or careless, cooperative or not.

Then we did a round of 'What was the purpose of that activity?' They understood that they were learning to work together and support each other.

We followed that with a straw–and–pin building activity. Some groups had more resources than others. We did that in 4s and then in 8s, each time discussing the strengths and weaknesses of their groups. Then I asked them to discuss the imbalance of resources, and what it means in other situations. We also talked about who took control in the groups. I asked them how their structures were like friendships. They talked it over and chose a spokesperson to report to the whole class. They came up with lots of relevant points.

Then I left them to choose groups and plan projects on environmental issues. At first they weren't that interested, some thought it had all been pointless. But even those very people began to come up with ideas. What was really good about it from my point of view was that everyone was involved, with one boy who is a bit intellectually disadvantaged, being a bit short of ideas, but still participating the whole time.

They're so convinced that they're stupid, and then they come up with fantastic and positive ideas. That was so exciting! Now they have a worm farm, they've created a permaculture garden, and they've been beautifying ugly areas. They paved one area, planted trees and vegetables in another spot. They've been working with the school gardener.

Sometimes, if someone's having a bad day, I don't send them to the office, I send them to our gardener. He listens to them, and they really talk to him, and then he puts them to work.

I'm trying so many new things. I think some people might say I'm not fully accountable. But the feedback from our admin team is just great, they really like what I'm doing. I record what each student has done, and the kids keep journals. They're not really overly keen about that, but they do it, every week, with an emphasis on what problems they had and how they solved them.

Two lessons a week are devoted to the project, and two are class work, which is assessed. So far, I've been setting the criteria, as they need to learn to negotiate their assessment. However, I haven't felt they were ready yet.

We planned a camp, and got it all set up. we called the timber company that owns the forest and got permission to camp in timberland. It was all organised with the school and the admin team. Then, just as we were about to go, some of the kids backed out. They said the surf was too good to miss, or they had other things to do. I was really disappointed, and everyone else felt let down. It just fizzled.

At that point, I came up to Perth to take part in the RASCL Conference, and felt inspired again. On the next Monday, we sat down and did two rounds: What annoyed you about this project? and What did you enjoy? When it was my turn to speak, I told them how disappointed I felt about the camp project not happening. They gave me lots of appreciation for trying to get it together, and that meant a lot to me. I think they learned something about commitment, because lots of kids were disappointed as well. After that, I found it was much easier for them to work in groups together.

DB comment: *I believe that Sarah has demonstrated a lot of important points here. How to get good learning out of disappointing outcomes. How to keep going when things get tough. How to work with students and consult them at every step of the way.*

Interview with Gemma Lawlor

Gemma is an art teacher at Bridgetown High School, who is, and has been from the beginning, a founding member and staunch supporter of RASCL (Regional Association for Student-Centred Learning). Her partner, John Eaton is also involved in our work in the same way. They both use games in their teaching, and they both run workshops for other teachers. At Bridgetown High School, a decision was made five years ago to become a student-centred school, and now the whole school has moved through the process of using sc methods carefully and gradually at first, and now with a fundamental student-centred approach throughout the school. In fact, they have moved past that point to a place where all of the current thinking on technology, accountability, student outcomes, and a new National Curriculum Framework are implemented in a student-centred manner, without question.

When I asked Gemma to talk to me about games, she made some initial points, and then spoke with great enthusiasm about two games which she has invented. They come under the category of Big Games, because they offer development in depth, length, and breadth.

Gemma speaking:

Yes, I use games all the time in my work, but I use them purposefully and carefully. I always debrief the games, because otherwise they are empty and meaningless. We have to talk about the content of the games, and also about the process. The students need time to think about what they've done. Teachers aren't trained to think this way for the most part, and either they don't take the time, or feel that they can't take it, to reflect with their kids on what they're doing. We also need to talk about how to apply the skills, and transfer them to other areas of the curriculum. Besides, we don't allow kids enough time to play as they had in their pre-school years. They need to play creatively, and construct their own meanings. I'll tell you about two of my favourite games.

Change Seats If …

This game is a variation of **How Do You Like Your Neighbour [p.56]**, in that there is always one seat less than there are people. When the initial statement is made, the people in question move across the circle to find a new seat. I take the game through three stages:

Stage One: Appearances (Literal)
Change seats if you wear blue socks.
Change seats if you are wearing a red T-shirt.
Change seats if you have full uniform on.

Stage Two: Likes and Dislikes (More abstract. Sharing Differences and Similarities.)
Change seats if you like the smell of leather.

Change seats if you like Chinese food.
Change seats if you ride horses.

Stage Three: Beliefs and Values (Abstract. More personal sharing.)
Change seats if you believe Cannabis should be legalised.
Change seats if you think SCL should be adopted by all schools.
At each stage, the leader gives the first two or three statements, and then the students or group members think up the rest.

So, that's the game. But it's the discussion afterwards that picks up the aims of the game, and identifies the learning involved.

'Honey, I Shrunk The Kids'

Introduction to the Game: The teacher comes to the lesson in role, holding a doll or puppet, perhaps an alien creature, and must take on the personality of that figure throughout the game. The teacher builds a story around it, and elaborates on who the figure is, and how he/she/it got there. The teacher might ask the students for some help in creating the figure's environment.

The students then have a square piece of paper, and they draw either the town or place where the figure lives, or construct a model of it.

The town where the doll lives

This basic plan can then be used to explore art, ecology, the environment, literature (e.g. Lilliput) or drawing to scale. You might discuss conflicts and the resolution of them, and also how you build a story with a beginning, a middle and an end. This game or lesson can take up as much or as little time as you want. I have played it for three hours at a conference, and I usually play it once a year in my classes, for several weeks.

Again, the students must have the chance to review what they've done, and to construct meaning from it.

Visitors

"A guest sees more in an hour than a host in a year."

Polish Proverb

When I was completing my M.Ed. at the University of Newcastle-upon-Tyne, I found myself working with a group of worn and tattered, unhappy school outcasts, known as 3L. They were seen as the scum of the school by staff and students alike, and tragically this is also how they saw themselves. In fact, I had asked the Principal for a class of average ability to work with, and he spitefully gave me 3L, for reasons which I never learned. I guessed it was because I was, in his eyes, a know-it-all psychologist from, of all heathen places, California, and he wanted to watch me flounder. Of course his assessment was pretty accurate, except that I didn't think I knew very much at all, and was scared right out of my tree. Also, I think I was given 3L because no one really cared whether they wasted 36 sessions with me. I should add that the school was considered the scum of the system, as well.

It was ironic that I was representing the Psychology Department, because I was actually working with Dorothy Heathcote, the larger than life authority on Drama in Education. A wonderful and controversial woman, and one of my most influential teachers. I was hypothesising that with the use of Drama and student-centred methods, I could enhance self-esteem in a group of children that I didn't previously know, and perhaps write about it in a way that would enable other teachers to do the same. But because Dorothy felt that self-esteem belonged in the Psychology Department, I went there for several consultations and found myself embroiled in questionnaire design, qualitative and quantitative research methods, and a control group.

In the end this was beneficial for me, because I ended up with an M.Ed. in Psychology, instead of the less 'academic' Drama. I told myself that if I tested both classes (3Y was considered an 'average' class, while 3L was the class from hell), I would be more than satisfied if the kids I actually taught showed an increase of ten per cent on my self-designed, self-esteem test (invalidated but approved by the Psychology Department).

The outcomes were miraculous. 3L showed a rise in self-esteem of 30 per cent, after only 36 lessons, many of which were interrupted and spoiled by outside forces. Some lessons were cancelled at the last minute because the kids all had to go to get their eyes tested or something, other times we would be told to meet in the Hall, and it would be closed, or there were carrots all over the floor after lunch and we had to go somewhere else. So all in all, I may have seen them for twenty lessons, some lasting half an hour, some, an hour and a half.

I have written about this in *The Hope Street Experience*, (Access Publishing, 1992, out of print but I have copies if anyone wants to look at one). So, I won't go into

35

aspects like The Hawthorn Effect, or the simple fact that they were getting some positive attention for a change. Nor will I go into detail about our first horrific lesson, in which I waited forty-five minutes for them to shut up and try to find out who I was and what I was doing there.

What I have been leading up to is the factor which I discovered by accident, and which I have since come to see as a definitive teaching approach, namely, *visitors*. Lesley Button wrote extensively about this, and it is after all only a variation on a time honoured method called Teacher-in-role. But I certainly thought at the time that I had invented it, and it is different, because the person visiting is a stranger to the group, and so the class only have the preconceptions that their own eyes reveal on first impression.

I confess to an ulterior (inferior?) motive for inviting my first visitors. I was terrified of being alone with that class. Like some other notable teachers, in classic books like *Up the Down Staircase*, and *To Sir with Love*, not to mention a lot of the late 90s teachers I meet in my work, I entered each day with shaking knees and sweaty face, heart pounding, and seeking survival above all else. The possibility of failing in my mission was looming of course, but there was an edge of incipient violence to the behaviour of about eight of those boys, and ultra sophisticated bitchiness to some of the girls, that meant I had to tough it out each day and stay cool most of the time while they threw their best blockades at me. Before and since, I have worked with many challenging classes full of alienated kids, but I can't remember ever feeling the kind of fear that 3L invoked.

So, in the second week I invited Chris, a Drama specialist that I knew, to visit the class in his well-known role as Albert the Tramp, as much to keep me company as anything else. To my surprise, Chris showed up in his usual clothes, told the kids who he actually was, went out and changed and came back in as a tramp. I never thought they would buy it, but they did. They suspended disbelief, and treated him at first as a smelly old tramp, that is, with sneers and revulsion. And then, wonder of wonders, when they saw how totally vulnerable he was, one of my incorrigible thirteen year olds offered him a stump of a cigarette, and someone else gave him a beat-up overcoat, and we were off and running. They cared for him, offered him tea, questioned him kindly, and when he began to mumble some answers, drew close without any remarks about his holey socks or his musty smell. Quite simply, they loved him. And I mean all of them, even Peter and Micky, my outstanding nemeses.

My research demanded that I carefully consider why this had transpired. I spent a goodly time questioning the kids about it but received inconclusive answers, so I tried again.

In fact, I invited a succession of visitors, one a week, including a famous Northern writer and fishmonger, who didn't come in role but told them stories about his childhood, on the quayside, a neighbourhood both streets and light years away from theirs. He told about his successful rise from poverty. The rule was, they could only get information from him by asking the right questions. And he could answer only what they asked.

Another day my youngest son rode into class on his motorbike, with black leather silver studded suit, helmet and goggles and vroomed right into the hall. They said they wanted to make a play about Hell's Angels, and they did, with my son as the key villain.

Another Drama teacher came in and we did a play about a bank robbery. It was probably the most successful project they attempted, and they were even into rehearsing it again and again to get it up to their own standards. By the way, in case you're worried about the morality of this, the Good Guys won!

One of the notable changes that was easily discernible was that they never sneered any more, no matter how startling the new apparition might be. They welcomed the person, sat down with him or her, and questioned them without rudeness till they found out what they needed to know, and then decided what they wanted to do.

What's this idea doing in a book of games? It is in a sense a game, since it has a set of rules to be discerned by the students, and some desired outcomes, and lots of action in between. However, I'm offering the visitor approach as a sound educational tool, because I have used it myself so successfully, and indeed have been the visitor on many occasions. Let's look at it more closely.

What were they learning? Readers, I ask you to ask yourselves that question before you continue. Make a list of what lessons in social skills and language they were taking in, as well as any others you can think of.

• • • • •

OK, thanks for the time out. Now here's what I thought and what 3L said. We all felt that the visitor approach had been a great success, that it was really exciting meeting these new people, and that the class had come together in a way they never had before.

Initially I had asked them what they did in their family when a visitor came. They said, for the most part, that the visitors were usually aunties and uncles or neighbours. Many of them were so familiar that they could walk in without knocking. Visits from strangers were rare. That their mother or father took care of them by making a cup of tea, or sometimes they made it for themselves. Tea was definitely *de rigueur*. But that's about all they knew, since they usually made themselves scarce unless it was someone they were very fond of.

So, we talked about the purpose of hospitality. Gratifyingly, by this time I could usually discuss things with them without too much interruption, if we had managed to find a quiet place to meet. They had very little experience of visiting anyone other than their families, or going over to a friend's house, so we had to imagine what it would be like to visit someone and be treated badly, or conversely to be met with hospitality. I later invited them over to my house for lunch, and they remembered exactly what to do as guests.

We were exploring social skills without sermonising. They learned how to start a conversation with someone new. How to help someone feel at home in a new place, and how to offer them food and drink. They began to be more polite to me and each other. I want to add here that I don't think much of manners and etiquette, I'm more concerned with consideration for other people, which they were beginning to display.

Visitors can be an injection of new life into the classroom, and they don't have to be exotic. I'm not suggesting that other teachers don't invite visitors in, but they mostly invite guests who are expert in a topic being studied, and not strictly for the visitor experience. With 'expert' visitors, rather than having the potential to be a completely open learning experience, there is an expectation about what the students should learn.

I don't want to underestimate the value of simply having another adult present in a difficult class, if the person knows how to work with these sorts of students. It means that team-teaching can happen, that groups can each have a leader. Also, from the point of view of practicality, one can take over if the other needs to leave the room for any reason.

An example of team-teaching is that when we worked on the play about the bank robbery, I took the robbers and we carefully planned strategies, while our visitor took the police to work out how they were going to lay their traps to catch the villains. A student teacher who was also with me took the customers to work out who each person was, how they would behave when desperate, and whether one of them would be a hero. We were able to use these three groups when rehearsing and performing.

But most of all, if the students are truly disadvantaged or difficult, there is just plain comfort in knowing that there is someone around to back you up. Also, in debriefing, the guest can often make very helpful observations which the teacher may have missed.

In summary, the visitor approach can achieve the following outcomes, if used thoughtfully and backed by expert questioning and discussion:

- meeting new people of types students don't usually see;
- understanding hospitality and welcome;
- enhancing group cohesiveness;
- backup for the teacher;
- improving concern for others;
- learning to use basic politeness of language;
- making lessons more exciting;
- leading up to Drama or writing;
- building synergy.

I'd like you to meet our visitor …

Notes

[1] Harris, Frank W. *Games*, Self published, 1982
[2] Skynner & Cleese *Life and How to Survive it*, London, Methuen, 1993
[3] Weinstein, Gerald and Fantini, Mario D. *Toward Humanist Education A Curriculum of Affect*, New York, Praeger Publishers, 1970
[4] Rogers, Carl *Client-Centred Therapy*, Boston, Houghton–Muffin, 1983
[5] Munby, Stephen *Assessing & Recording Achievement*, Oxford, Basil Blackwell, 1989

Chapter Two

Big Games for Big Game Hunters

Unpacking Some of the Bigger Games

We are using the term 'unpacking' as a metaphor. The game arrives on your doorstep like a gift, with a set of instructions, but the playing instructions are not adequate for a detailed understanding of the game. Some of the games are big, in the sense that they can be played and then developed, and perhaps may last for a number of days, even weeks, as they grow and meld with the curriculum subjects or with work projects.

For these sorts of activities then, the teacher or leader may need a much deeper sense of what the concepts involved are really about, and how the growth may happen.

AMERICAN CHARADES

"A man shows his character by what he laughs at."

Old German Proverb

There is some confusion between the Old English game of Charades ('A' as in Father), and the more recent American game of Charades (rhymes with crusades), seen played in the British celebrity game show *Give us a Clue*.

The subtle but crucial difference between the two versions is to do with the ultimate purpose of the game. In Old Charades, the teams dress up in costumes and act out the syllables of a word, for example, come-you-nick-ate-shun for 'Communication'. The object is to have a lovely time acting out the word, while making it as difficult as possible for the other team to guess what it is. In other words, the aim is to befuddle the enemy!

In American Charades, the object is to work with your own team and communicate as effectively as possible to them the name of a play, book or song, etc. In other words, to use synergy to be faster and smarter than the other team. In this chapter, 'Charades' refers to the American version.

Since we are staunch advocates of non-competitive games, why would we include such a fiercely competitive game, which often includes – in fact *should* include – shouting and avidly seeking to win? In fact, I have to admit that although I am normally among the gentlest and least competitive of gamesters, I go mad and become a cutthroat during Charades with my own friends.

The reason we have chosen to include Charades in this book is that in many ways it is the most exciting and growthful group game to be found, and is truly a team-building exercise.

The game
Each team must first work together to write down the topics to be guessed. They must decide on the level of difficulty which would be both fair and challenging for the other team. They must search their combined store of knowledge for suitable titles, quotes and famous names. When play begins, everyone must focus on the actor, and watch very carefully, listening all the time to the guesses of the other players.

The secret of being a successful actor in Charades is to get yourself organised. It does not require you to be an accomplished thespian, however, it does require that you think through what you are going to do, very carefully, *before the stop watch starts*. Think about key words. Think of words that rhyme with the ones in your title and will be easier to act out. Think what gestures and movements you will use as clues for your team, in short, be well prepared before you start.

For example, say the movie you are going to act out is *Butch Cassidy and the Sundance Kid*. You would think about the fact that 'Butch' and 'Cassidy' would be hard to act, while 'Sundance' and 'Kid' would be easy. So, you would signal for the fifth word, and divide the word Sundance, giving the symbol for two syllables, then act out 'Sun', and act out 'dance'. This is what is meant by a key word, because by this time someone will probably have guessed the movie title. If not, you could go to the sixth word and give the symbol for 'sounds like' and act out 'lid', while the team shouts out words that rhyme, like bid, did, rid, mid, till they come to 'Kid'.

Meanwhile, your team should *focus*, watch, listen and guess. When they shout out ideas you will need to signal when they are getting warm, when they are off the track completely, or if they've got it exactly on the nose. Consequently you are having to act, concentrate, listen, and feedback, concurrently.

Both teams can take delight in the ingenuity and creative prowess of the actors. Both teams can listen and learn, if they stay focused. Beyond all that, the most satisfying thing about Charades for me is watching people develop self-confidence and get better at playing it.

When I was teaching middle school, I had seven classes a day. Every Friday each of the classes played Charades for about half an hour, if they chose it. Of course this was a sly ruse on my part, because it satisfied my Charades obsession. But in every case, the students developed their skills and confidence by leaps and bounds. Soon they were haunting the library and their bookshelves at home to find appropriate titles and ideas. They knew how to organise themselves in every phase of the game. They got very excited, and were thrilled by the success of both teams. They learned to support each other and to be what we used to call 'good sports', meaning simply that they could create a win–win situation out of a competitive game. They felt that they were learning a lot.

People weren't teased or blamed for mistakes or slowness. Their gestures and movements became clearer to read. They became more efficient at the game, and they learned to be economical, to persist, and to work hard. They laughed with each other, which had a healing and unifying effect. We could have joined a national competition, if there had been such a thing. I regret I didn't start one myself!

Process

The player can think as long as they want before giving the signal to the timekeeper that they are ready to begin. Once the timing starts, try not to take time out for thinking, that should be done before you start. The team gets three minutes to guess, and their time is added up by the scorekeeper as the game progresses. As in golf, the lowest score wins.

The order of acting and guessing is:

Category
How many words in the title
Word number to guess first
How many syllables in that word
Syllable to be done first, if appropriate

Then you're off and running, using whatever words and symbols you may need to keep your team on track. Encourage everyone to take part, and have fun!

Symbols

Book	create open book with two hands
Film	winding motion represents camera turning
Song	two hands around open mouth
Play	two hands pulling curtain
Opera/Musical	song plus pulling curtain motion
Saying, proverb, quotation	one finger making rolling motion away from mouth
Famous woman	curtsey
Famous man	bow
Name	pat top of head with open hand
'The'	form a T with two forefingers
Little word	thumb and forefinger indicate little space (then team guesses, of, at, for, to, by, on, in, is, it, etc.)
Whole idea	use two forefingers to make shape of world globe
Sounds like	fingers pull on earlobe (then act out rhyming word, like 'lid' for 'kid', while team guesses, as above, did, rid, bid, lid, KID!)
On the right track, keep going	circling motion with hand
Not on the right track	thumbs down
Forget it completely	sweep hands sideways
Right on	forefinger on nose, or thumbs up
	Over the years we've developed other categories, depending on the sophistication of the group playing, e.g.
Famous diseases	hands clutching throat
Famous recipes	stirring in a bowl motion

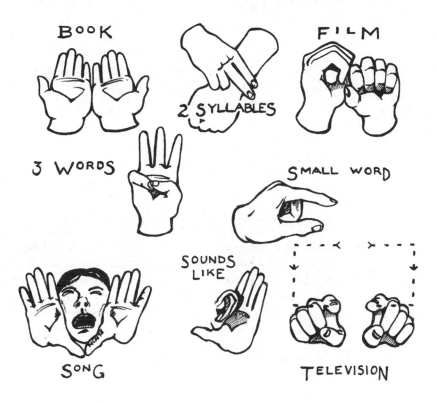

The use of these symbols quickly and correctly is very important, and the actor must pay close attention to the team's guesses, listen and point to the right guesser, while giving the 'on the nose' or 'thumbs up' sign. Symbols should always be reviewed by the leader before the game starts, if playing with a new group.

BIG BOSS

AIMS: Thinking and talking under pressure, memory, physical movement, fun, awareness of management issues.

MATERIALS: None.

PROCEDURE:
1. The group sits in a circle.
2. The leader chooses one group member at random and tells them that they are sitting in the Big Boss's seat.
3. Then, in a clockwise direction around the circle, the other members of the company are named, in reverse hierarchical order, e.g. Company Director 1, Company Director 2, Company Director 3, Managing Director 1, 2 and 3, Accountant 1, 2 and 3, and so on through the company to Secretaries, Caretakers, Workers, the final two are always Tea-lady and Toilet Cleaner.
4. The size of the group is immaterial as characters can be added or subtracted with ease.
5. The game always begins with the Big Boss who starts off by saying "Big Boss to Accountant 1" (for example), who in turn must begin the next round by addressing someone else, e.g. "Accountant 1 to Secretary" and so on. You cannot pass the turn back to the person who originally addressed you.
6. If any mistake is made, such as hesitation, mispronunciation or wrong name called, then the culprit is 'demoted' and becomes 'Toilet Cleaner'.
7. The person making the mistake must vacate their chair and sit on the Toilet Cleaner's chair. Their vacated chair is then taken by the next person on the right, whose vacated chair is taken by the next person to their right and so on.
8. Therefore, after each mistake, some members of the group always get 'promoted'.
9. The game finishes after a suitable period of time (minimum 15 minutes).

VARIATIONS: Use 'Unemployed' rather than Toilet Cleaner. Use other forms of hierarchies, e.g. Hindu caste system, armed forces, school management structures, etc. Play the game in a foreign language.

SOURCE: John Norris

BIG BOSS UNPACKED

I have known groups to play this game for over an hour. It requires a very high level of concentration and taxes one's memory. It is a game played at speed and can be quite demanding. It is also a game which contains many hidden assumptions worthy of reflection and discussion. Whilst the group is sitting in an apparently egalitarian circle, it is obvious that a hierarchy is present. Also, there is a gender assumption in 'Tea-lady' and if any group failed to question this, I would want to discuss why! A discussion debrief after the game can lead into many fertile areas relating to issues of management and organisation.

A simple starting point is to ask which members of the group found it hardest to concentrate or remain committed throughout the game. More often than not, we tend to find that those members of the group at the 'higher' end of the hierarchy tend to concentrate the hardest as they have their apparent position to maintain. Conversely, a few members may have found themselves relatively stuck at the lower end. Did they find their levels of concentration and commitment dwindling as the game unfolded? Usually the answer is 'Yes'. I have used this to open up all kinds of issues within organisations, e.g. the impact of continuous failure on one's levels of motivation and performance.

Similarly, are all members of the group seeking to become the Big Boss? Is this a realistic aim for all members of the organisation/company? If not, why not? A similar line of questioning can lead to a discussion on whether it is likely that the hierarchy is based on meritocratic principles or not.

Skilful questioning can take these issues further still. Who are likely to be the most ambitious members of the company? Big Boss? Not necessarily so, as apparently they have already 'arrived'. Company Directors? Would they wish to maintain the *status quo* at all costs? Or, would the middle-managers who are already well-established in the hierarchy, be looking both ways?

Similarly, issues of trust and integrity can be explored. I have often used blunt questioning to elicit responses, sometimes asking, "Who is most likely to steal from this company?" The nature of the responses can reveal fascinating 'mindsets' about participants' views of hierarchies and the nature of organisations.

I have found Big Boss to be a particularly useful tool to promote issues of the working environment with school leavers or those about to embark on work-experience programs. Similarly, I have used the game with adults, to release creative energies relating to management structures within their organisations. The simplicity of the game and the randomness of position within the company allows an expression of viewpoints to take place in a much more general and honest fashion, allowing us to get to the 'guts' of these crucial issues.

THE COUNTING GAME

AIMS: Teamwork, self-pacing, listening, leadership.

MATERIALS: None.

PROCEDURE:
1. The group sits in a circle.
2. The leader counts those present (including themself). No one has any particular value.
3. The leader explains to the group that the purpose of the game is for the group to count to___ (the total number in group) with only one person shouting out a number at any one time.
4. The group cannot point or shout out in the order that they sit.
5. Anyone can say any number but if more than one person shouts the same number they must go back to 1.

VARIATIONS: None.

NOTES: This activity is particularly effective with a new group. It gets exciting towards the end. For discussion/evaluation – Acting individually and working as a team. Leadership skills. How did individuals act? What makes a good team player?

SOURCE: John Norris

THE COUNTING GAME UNPACKED

The following is an account of one lesson that began with **The Counting Game**, which built group trust and laid the foundation for a very rewarding group discussion.

This particular class is made up of thirty mixed-ability boys and girls, aged between 13 and 14. A lively group of youngsters, that I work with for one hour a week, on a Thursday afternoon. The lesson which was observed was the fourth one of the year. During the previous three, we had worked with no subject context as such, as I had concentrated on developing a positive ethos with a high level of personal interaction. Therefore, I had employed games such as **Big Boss [p.46]**, **One to Nine [p.60]** and **Famous Films [p.54]** to facilitate this. There had been a considerable amount of laughter within the group, and I was pleased with the group's overall development.

The lesson observed was to be the first of a series on 'human relations' which would include sex education. I had already decided to proceed as normal, with several light hearted exercises to facilitate laughter and create a general feeling of well being. In recent years, I have come to appreciate the importance of laughter in calming a lively class. This may seem a contradiction in terms, but experience suggests otherwise. At this point, it is well worth considering the different types of laughter that can occur within a group. Clearly, there is nervous laughter, often based on fear. This can be linked to sarcasm, insults or any of the other self-defeating control mechanisms. Essentially then, its function is defensive. Similarly, groups can use aggressive laughter as a means of establishing hierarchies, or to show disapproval of a situation. Its essence is rejection. The kind of laughter I try to promote might best be described as 'mirth' or a celebration of the comical, it is essentially good humoured, and is a shared awareness of our infallibility. This type of laughter is powerful medicine indeed.

Laughter releases tension, helps calm the nervous system, and used with skill can be a catalyst for very serious and thoughtful work. Therefore, by combining a light hearted activity with a game of physical movement the group had relaxed, and the atmosphere was one of expectancy.

In addition, the new seating arrangement had helped to break down any established peer groups which might have formed prior to the lesson. I began by re-capping on the agreed rules for performing a round, i.e. that it is perfectly OK to 'pass' and that no interruptions are allowed (something I find particularly difficult!). My experience tells me that this basic technique is indicative of a change in ownership, which pupils come to internalise quickly. Once this happens, new norms are established (this is *our* lesson) and behaviour modification takes place (I will listen to you).

My approach to a round is essentially two-fold. Firstly, I am never perplexed if large numbers 'pass' – especially on difficult issues and questions. I believe it is vital that the group leader's body posture, eye-contact, and facial expression reflects this – it is OK to pass. Secondly I *never* interrupt, and I really do mean *never*. I do not own the round. We all own the round, of course, I challenge, question, and attempt to clarify many of the viewpoints expressed, but only *after* the round is completed. The message is obvious. Everyone is of equal value. Which of course is not the same as saying that every possible opinion is of equal value, as there can be racist, sexist remarks and so on. These of course can be challenged by any group member.

As a group performs a round, the ability for all members to *listen* effectively is crucial, especially for the group leader. There are two main reasons for this. The first is that we send a powerful message to individuals when we demonstrate active listening skills – literally 'I am hearing what you have to say'. Secondly, the group leader must 'store up' the various points of view, in order to introduce constructive questioning during the next part of the process – the inevitable debate and discussion.

Therefore, at the end of the round, direct questioning of individuals may be appropriate. I believe it is worth thinking very seriously about the issue of effective questioning. My experience of working with groups indicates that open-ended questioning can be particularly productive in engaging positive responses. For example, I am much more likely to use, "Emily, can you help me understand your point a little more, by telling us what you meant by … ?" or even throw out a controversial question such as "When is it OK to lie?" which tends to elicit quick-fire responses, than I am to use the closed type of question which can often be used like an offensive weapon, "David, will you please justify your opinion to the rest of the group?" This contains the threat message – 'I do not like what you have said'. I believe that we must consciously avoid such control mechanisms if we are to truly engage the creativity of young (and old) minds.

From the group leader's point of view of course, an open-ended approach can lead to an apparent lack of control. However, my idea of the perfect lesson is when I become little more than a conductor for their orchestra!

Here is an example of what can happen with this particular group of young people. The round had begun with a very open-ended question, "Is it better to be in love with someone before having a sexual relationship?" Quite a few members of the group had passed and some students had made very insightful comments. Gender difference had been mentioned by some, and challenged by others. It seemed that gender differences most interested the group, consequently I focused on this in the discussion phase.

It was a group decision, rather than my own, to enter the world of family relationships. However, it became clear within ten minutes, that students were talking about very personal matters indeed.

It is worth reflecting at this point, on the issues of trust and confidentiality when dealing with such sensitive issues. During this particular session I felt that I needed to elaborate on our situation, before allowing the discussion to develop further. Firstly, I think it is highly appropriate to establish the parameters of trust, when dealing with any kind of personal disclosure within a group. I was quite frank, and asked the group what we should do. The collective decision was that any personal statements would be confidential to the group. I have no doubt that each student will have kept their word on this. Secondly, as a professional with responsibility for my group's welfare, it is vital that students should know the limits to my promise of confidentiality, i.e. that it exists within a legal framework, and that I would always be professionally bound to disclose information, if I thought a young person were at serious risk. My experience tells me that this is not usually a problem for a group.

Therefore, with the parameters clearly established I was happy to let the discussion move in this direction. Personally, I feel quite humbled when young people place their trust in each other and in the group leader, and allow themselves to talk about issues which are personal and important in their lives. Separation, divorce, violence, unhappiness within the family, were the experiences of quite a significant number of the students. I suspect that for some of them, this had been one of their first opportunities to externalise their feelings. Many group leaders would be rightfully cautious about the dangers of this kind of work, and indeed I would never contrive a session in such a way as to force members to talk so personally. However, if a discussion moved into such an area and the group was happy with it, I would go with it.

The general conclusions I would draw from my experience of the lesson are:

- it is important to develop a group identity prior to embarking upon sensitive issues;
- there is a need to modify the peer group;
- there is a relationship between humour and serious discussion;
- there is a need for active listening and effective questioning to promote discussion and participation;
- it is important to establish the boundaries of trust and confidentiality.

Here is some feedback on the lesson from the students' journals: (Initials protect the children's identity)

Our PSE (personal and social education) groups have only been working for 3 weeks (3 hours), but there is a sense of trust between everyone. In one of our lessons we started by having a bit of a laugh, and then we had a discussion about family problems and relationships. Everyone went serious and I think it was because nearly everyone has had something like a divorce happen in their family, or some other problem. At the end of the lesson we all agreed not to tell anyone about anything we had discussed during the lesson. I think it worked because people in the group respect each other.
S C and E S

I was in the lesson and Mr Norris said we could have another game of **The Counting Game**, we had completed it the week before. This week we completed it at the second attempt, then we had a talk about how we managed to play the game. Some people said it was the pause between the numbers but I thought it was because the group wanted to complete it. Then we played the laughing game [**Laughter is the best Medicine p.144**], we had good fun. Then we started talking about problems at home and people were talking about things they wouldn't usually talk about, I think we managed to do this because we all made a promise not to tell anyone outside the group, I think it was all based on trust.
K R

Some people may wonder how we could be playing games one minute and having serious discussion the next, but for us it came naturally, which was weird as we had only had 3 hour long lessons together. To begin with there was a bit of tension and slight unwillingness to talk but as the lesson drew on we found ourselves telling the class personal things which we had only told our closest friends. We had all made a promise not to repeat anything anyone had said which helped us to express our feelings on the topic truthfully and without worry that anyone was going to laugh at us. At the end of the lesson we found it difficult to find a good place to end the discussion as each topic of conversation led to another.
M W

To start the lesson we played some games and introduced ourselves to each other. When you first meet someone there is a fair amount of tension, so it relaxed the situation to play games. Everybody relaxed and started talking to each other a lot more. We played a game which involved people waiting, taking their time and listening. This was **The Counting Game**. It was interesting to see who went first.

After the games everyone felt they knew and could trust each other enough so that we could move on to much deeper and more personal topics. We all made a promise to each other and respected each other's opinions.
H T

FAMOUS FILMS

AIMS: Memory, listening, teamwork, discussion, fun, group integration, breaking down cliques and gender groups, brainstorm new ideas, movement.

MATERIALS: Pen and paper for the leader.

PROCEDURE:
1. The leader names a category (later group members can choose categories relevant to their subject or organisational needs).
2. One by one, the members come to the leader and whisper an example of that category, e.g. with films, *Jurassic Park*. No one else must hear what they whisper. The leader writes them down in random order, for his/her eyes only.
3. Form even groups, approximately 1/4 the size of the full group (e.g. with 20 people, groups of 5, etc). Move into small group circles spaced out around the room.
4. When everyone has given the leader their example the leader reads the entire list for the first time. Players must stay silent and not let on when their's is read out. IMPORTANT – Never let on or tell anyone what your example is.
5. The spokesperson from group 1 begins by making a claim, e.g. "The person who chose Jurassic Park is in Group 2". If this is correct, the person whose example was Jurassic Park is captured from Group 2 and must join Group 1. Group 1 can continue to make claims until they get one wrong. If the claim is wrong, whichever group was chosen has a turn (Group 2 in this case).
6. Each group in their turn must capture a 'new person', before they can re-capture those already guessed and captured.
7. Eventually there will only be one group left.

VARIATIONS: In an adult organisation, topics could be relevant, e.g. Ways of improving your organisation, products, cosmetics, food, marketing ideas. Careers instead of films. Famous people in history. Animals. Play it in another language.

NOTES: Do not attempt to carry this game over to another day – it must be finished. This is much more than a warm up – it sounds complicated but it is worth it. Can last one hour. Can be based on curriculum subject. Gets exciting towards the end. Keep reminding groups that they can only have one spokesperson.

SOURCE: John Norris

FAMOUS FILMS UNPACKED

This is a useful activity for new groups as it encourages a high degree of social interaction and communication. The group is purposefully engaged in a non-threatening environment, allowing contributions from all members. Scraps of personal knowledge can be usefully employed when guesses are being made. With a large group, it becomes a considerable task to remember the complete list, and hence encourages active listening. There is physical movement from group to group, with attendant advantages already discussed.

HOW DO YOU LIKE YOUR NEIGHBOUR?

AIMS: Exercise, warm-up, fun.

MATERIALS: Chairs.

PROCEDURE:
1. Place chairs in a circle.
2. Number each person 1, 2, 3, 4, etc.
3. One person stands in the centre and one chair is removed.
4. The person in the centre points to someone and says, "How do you like your neighbour?" There are two ways to answer:
   a) "I like him." In this case, everyone gets up and moves to another chair. Last one standing is in the centre next.
   b) "I don't like him." In this case, the centre person asks, "Who do you want? ❶ " The answerer calls any two numbers – the two people on their right and left must move, and the two people with the numbers called must try to get their chairs.
   ❶ If when asked "Who do you want?", the answerer says: "Nobody", then everyone except the answerer runs around the outside of the circle, until the answerer says, "Stop". Everyone then goes for a chair.

VARIATIONS: Invent new answers with the group.

SOURCE: Donna Brandes

HOW DO YOU LIKE YOUR NEIGHBOUR UNPACKED

Recently a group of teachers on a training course were seated in a circle, working intensively on SCL skills. They were looking very tired and 'Friday afternoon-ish', so we thought we might play an active game. Remembering that changing other people's moods could be quite manipulative, we asked them if they noticed how tired people in the group were looking, and a cry of "TIRED!" went up. They acknowledged that they felt they had reached the ends of their intellectual energy, and would like to move around a bit.

At the mention of an active game, they sat up and came to life. It was then very easy to start playing How do you like your Neighbour, as we were already in position, and everyone was keen to play. We always start out with one rule at a time, and then add two or three others, from the original game, ending up by asking the group to think up new rules. One new rule they invented was:

Centre person   "How do you like your neighbour?" (Pointing to someone)
Reply   "I like them to be around."

In which case everyone has to get up and run around their chair before crossing the circle to get a new chair. Another rule that we particularly like is:

Centre person   "How do you like your neighbour?" (Pointing to someone)
Reply   "I just love them."

Everyone then has to get up and hug someone before they can run for a chair. If you feel that hugs are inappropriate for a certain group, you could perhaps use handshakes.

Of course, How do you like your neighbour is in common with other games like Musical Chairs, Fruit Salad, Wave the Ocean and more, in that they all operate with one less chair than there are people, so that someone always ends up in the centre of the circle. However, we don't think that this makes the game fall into the competitive category, because whoever it is in the middle is only there for a minute, and there is no ultimate winner or loser.

Neighbour is also one of those games that can have the dual effect of calming the group down, and enlivening them. When asked what the aims of the game were, and why they might play it with their classes, the group of teachers said:

- it woke us up and got the circulation going;
- it cleared my head for more thinking;
- I was feeling fidgety, it blew off some excess energy;
- you have to constantly be alert and ready to move;
- you have to remember the rules, and invent new ones;
- you have to listen;
- you have to be very careful.

This last comment raised a very important point. Some students, and even grown-ups, will take advantage of crossing the circle, seeing it as an opportunity to stomp someone or push them. This possibility alone stops many leaders from choosing the game. But you could look at it as a perfect opportunity for safety training.

One way to do this is to stop the game immediately when any 'foul play' occurs, and the next time the group asks to play it, start a discussion on what went wrong last time? Ask the group to put some agreements into operation, specifically for games which involve racing for chairs. Make sure that everyone has agreed on rules which ensure a safe environment; participants should pace themselves, look out for each other, and not touch anyone, except within the rules. If anyone breaks an agreement, the game stops immediately, and doesn't go on until the next meeting. This has to constitute part of the agreements.

PIG, WOLF AND FARMER

(An ancient game revisited)

AIMS: Fun, team game, strategy, group interaction.

MATERIALS: None.

PROCEDURE:
1. The group splits into two teams which face each other. There are three choices – pig, wolf, and farmer, and the leader explains that pig takes wolf, wolf takes farmer, and farmer takes pig.
2. Each team huddles to decide which one of the three they wish to be and when they have decided they face the other team again.
3. The three choices have different signs:
   pigs   wiggle both index fingers either side of their head
   wolves   display their sharp claws
   farmers   perform a digging action
4. At the count of three, both teams move towards each other and display their action.
5. There is a points system and whichever team 'takes' the other, (as described above) wins a point.

Pig, Wolf and Farmer ... Piggies win again!

58

VARIATIONS: Each team works out five 'plays' in advance. Capture one person from the other team each time you win. Three teams and three different ways of gaining points. For young children use Fairies, Wizards, and Witches as the choices. For Social Studies, use relevant figures from history, or current events like Hunters, Foxes, Conservationists. Use a variety of animals from the food chain. For adults in the business world, use rival companies, or factions within companies. Have people invent their own teams.

PIG, WOLF AND FARMER UNPACKED

Here is a variation on a very old game, known in the past as Paper, Scissors and Rock. We don't know how old it is, but we can imagine cave men around a fire, challenging each other with grunts of triumph and disgust. Players put their hands behind their backs, chant 'One, two, three', and thrust a hand out flat for paper, two fingers in scissors shape for scissors, or a fist for rock. The winner is determined according to the following rules: Paper covers Rock, Rock breaks Scissors, Scissors cut Paper. The game is amazingly simple, so why has it lasted so long? Well, it's portable, it's quick to play, and requires no preparation time. It's usually played in pairs or threes, though you could invent a more complicated version. It's instantly decided. Played at its best, it requires strategic thinking, as each player tries to guess what the other will do next.

Pig, Wolf and Farmer, is noisier, involves more movement and is a team game. It's one of the few competitive games we've offered. It has all the advantages of the earlier version, needing no preparation or materials. The important thing is, people seem to love it. We have seen even the most dignified group of academics or entrepreneurs, unwind and play this one. As with all the games, the really juicy bit, as far as learning goes, comes in the debriefing. Some questions for participants to consider:

- When you went into the huddle, who was the leader?
- Was the leader consulting the others, or dominating them?
- Did you make your decisions by consensus or were some people passive?
- Did you spend any time guessing what the other team would do?
- Would you describe the atmosphere within your huddle as competitive or cooperative?
- What do you think the aims of the game are?
- Were they achieved?

The leader needs to remember that for questions like these, there are no wrong answers. All ideas should be accepted equally. It might be appropriate to discuss these questions in a round – unless the group is very large.

ONE TO NINE

AIMS: Communication, problem-solving, teamwork, leadership skills.

MATERIALS: Nine chairs. Nine numbered cards (optional). Nine pieces of paper numbered one to eight.

PROCEDURE: 1. Arrange the chairs as follows:

        ③   ②   ①

        ④   ⑤   ⑥

        ⑨   ⑧   ⑦

2. Each chair is given a number as in the above sequence. The leader may wish to place a card on each chair, or simply give verbal instructions as to the number of each chair.

3. Eight volunteers sit in numbers one to eight at random. Number nine is left empty to begin with, but of course the number of the empty chair will be changing all the time.

4. The leader shuffles the numbered pieces of paper and then randomly distributes them to the eight participants.

5. The object is for each member to end up in the seat indicated on their piece of paper.

6. To accomplish this participants may move, horizontally and vertically into an empty chair, but never diagonally. Neither may participants swap chairs or numbers. If you look at the diagram above you will see that only number 4 or number 8 could move first. Suppose number 4 moves to chair 9 leaving chair 4 empty. Then only 3 or 5 could move, and so the play continues.

7. The activity finishes when all eight participants are sitting in the correct chairs, or after a set time limit.

VARIATIONS: Match historical events to dates or characters. Use chronologies or sequences to reinforce memory. Communicate in a foreign language. Play the game in silence. Use observers to feedback to participants.

SOURCE: John Norris

ONE TO NINE UNPACKED

We like this game for many reasons. It is an excellent ice-breaker, and sets a purposeful target for group members. It is largely non-threatening with positive outcomes. It encourages effective verbal communication, and by using an observer who takes notes, feedback can be given to both individuals and groups, on the strategies employed. It quickly establishes a group identity, without relying on potentially complex verbal introductions and social interaction.

The team spirit, so quickly established, may then be productively engaged on a follow up activity or task. This activity immediately encourages flexibility of habit and behaviour. The physical dimensions of the game, in terms of spacial awareness and movement, help challenge our fixed notions of territory which can restrict creativity and the power to change. In so many walks of life we find ourselves 'stuck' in certain positions from which we find it difficult to move. This is often reflected in the fixed layout of the office and classroom.

It is our contention that physical movement is a much underrated tool for personal and collective development. Our own childhood experiences should remind us of the potentially liberating effect of physical movement on our sense of well-being. As educators and trainers, we believe that such techniques should form an integral part of development programmes.

SIMILARITIES AND DIFFERENCES
(Affectionately known as 'Squiggles')

AIMS: Introduction, self-awareness, classification, listening, cooperation.

MATERIALS: Sheet of paper and pencil for each group.

PROCEDURE: 1. Draw these five shapes for the whole group to see using two different colours.

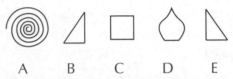

2. Ask the students to divide them into groups according to their similarities and differences. For example:
All five figures can be drawn with a single line. (5–0)
Two figures are triangles, three are not. (2–3)
Three are red, two are blue. (3–2)

NOTE: You are NOT permitted to have a 4–1 grouping, because that leaves one figure alone.

3. Players form groups of five.

4. The leader tells them that the same rules will apply to groupings as above, 5–0, 3–2 or 2–3 are allowed, 4–1 groups are not.

5. Each group elects a scribe, to write down the ideas.

6. Groups begin to group themselves according to the following categories:
Stage One: Appearances. The leader stresses, no negative comments! e.g. "Three of us have glasses, two don't." (The scribe need only record the main idea – glasses) But NOT, "Three of us are gorgeous, two are ugly."
Stage Two: Ideas and Tastes. e.g. one person might say they love Italian food. If at least one more person agrees, then the scribe writes it down. But not if the speaker is left alone. One person might say, I like the new curriculum framework, etc.
Stage Three: Values and Feelings. e.g. "What I value in a friend is a good sense of humour." Or, "I feel sick when I read about youth suicide."

7. When all three rounds are finished, the leader says that the next group task is to find something unique about their group, that no other group could say.

8. The leader asks the groups to write down what they think the aims of the game are.
9. All groups come together for discussion and sharing.

VARIATIONS: If played in the staff room, ask teachers to come up with applications for this game to every subject in the curriculum; after all, it is about classifications. Use in any subject, e.g. Management: classification of tasks and roles. Biology: classification of species. Give out photos, and the groups classify them according to physical characteristics of mammals, reptiles, etc. Maths: classification of numbers, prime, odd, even, depending on the group's age level. This game is seminal, because it can be applied to any subject in the curriculum, as well as to social studies.

SOURCE: Donna Brandes

SIMILARITIES AND DIFFERENCES UNPACKED

This is an excellent opening game. If you play it with a group, it is mandatory to stop in time to allow for debriefing. I usually ask at least three questions:

a) What are the aims of this game?
b) How can you connect it to our work?
c) What other categories could the groups explore?

People usually tell me that the aims are; getting to know people, learning to accept different ideas and values and controlled self-disclosure. Whatever the group says in answer to these questions, or any others you might ask, the discussion is just about as important as the game itself.

One of the great things about this game is that it can be played with any number of people from five on up to hundreds, as long as you can move people into groups of five. The main benefit is that I have never seen it fail as a warm-up, and even groups that seem to be hostile and non-receptive to begin with always seem to enjoy it.

THE X Y GAME

AIMS: Communication, teamwork, cooperation, devising game plans, life philosophy.

MATERIALS: Copies of the scoring system (given below).

3 pairs per cluster	
3 Xs	Lose 1 point each
2 Xs	Win 1 point each
1 Y	Lose 2 points
1 X	Win 2 points
2 Ys	Lose 1 point each
3 Ys	Win 1 point each .

4 pairs per cluster	
4 Xs	Lose 1 point each
3 Xs	Win 1 point each
1 Y	Lose 3 points
2 Xs	Win 2 points each
2 Ys	Lose 2 points each
1 X	Win 3 points
3 Ys	Lose 1 point each
4 Ys	Win 1 point each

		Time Allowed	With	Choice X or Y	Points Won/Lost	Balance
Round	1	2 minutes	partner			
	2	1 minute	partner			
	3	1 minute	partner			
Bonus round score × 3		2 minutes	cluster			
	4	1 minute	partner			
	5	1 minute	partner			
	6	1 minute	partner			
Bonus round score × 5		3 minutes	cluster			
	7	1 minute	partner			
	8	1 minute	partner			
	9	1 minute	partner			
Bonus round score × 10		3 minutes	cluster			
	10	1 minute	partner			

PROCEDURE: 1.   Groups of 8 or 6 – called a 'cluster'. Seated as follows:

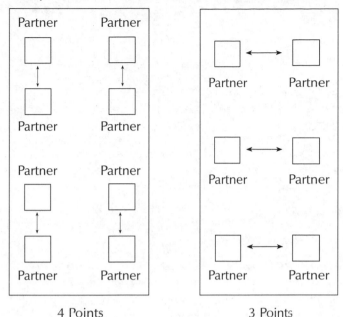

4 Points   3 Points

Each member of the cluster has a partner, who sits opposite. Each cluster should sit within close physical proximity to one another (as above).

2. No one may leave their chair at any time.

3. The leader explains that after each round, pairs will jointly decide whether to record an X or a Y under the choice column. During most rounds, the rule is that only partners may communicate. However, in rounds 4, 7 and 10, the whole cluster may communicate. However, there should be no communication *between* clusters at any time.

4. The scoring system will become self-evident. However, at no time should the leader indicate the purpose of the game. Allow each pair to work out their own strategy, and the leader offers neither encouragement nor criticism after each round but simply enforces the rules of pair and cluster communication.

5. At the end of each round, the leader should check the scores.

6. The game finishes after round 10.

VARIATIONS: None.

SOURCE: John Norris

THE X Y GAME UNPACKED

After the initial perplexed reactions to the scoring system, participants quickly develop their own strategies and responses to the game. One of the first reactions, of course, is the quest to find the 'winner'. I usually attempt to surprise the participants by stating afterwards that the game was a competition, between clusters, rather than between pairs within a cluster. Therefore, negative or positive scores can then be added up, and each cluster can be given a final tally.

A key area, of course, is an examination of the issue of individual versus organisational or group 'success'. Some pairs may have adopted a ruthless 'I win, you lose' strategy, others may have developed a 'win–win' strategy, albeit by sacrificing particularly high individual scores. Others may have lapsed into a 'lose–lose' mode, in frustration at the strategies of other members of the cluster. This is fertile ground indeed for discussion.

Debriefing should concentrate on teasing out some of those issues. What is the likely impact on organisational performance if members operate on the 'I win, you lose' mode? Robin Skynner would suggest an inability to respond positively to change, and a lower level of effective decision-making. Some strategies, may of course, have included a high degree of broken promises, if not downright cheating. Whilst this might have proved amusing within the context of the game (having said that, I have seen genuine anger erupt too!), discuss the effect this has on decision-making and successful interpersonal relationships within an organisation.

Such issues of trust permeate the hidden agendas of all organisations, whether classrooms, business enterprises or rehabilitation programs. It is our belief that effective target-setting, action-planning and systems of appraisal can become sterile operations, unless the certainty of trust is established.

Chapter Three

Games

Section One

Self-esteem and Communication

AMAZING EVENTS

AIMS: Sharing, fun, enhance self-esteem.

MATERIALS: Pen and paper.

PROCEDURE:
1. Participants think of an amazing event from their lives. The game works much better with real events, but if someone can't think of one, they can make one up, that they wish would have really happened.
2. They write the event on a numbered card, in just a few sentences, disguising their handwriting and not signing them.
3. The cards are then read along with the numbers.
4. Participants guess who wrote each one.
5. After the people have been matched with the cards they can elaborate and share their experiences, and say how their lives were affected by the event.

VARIATIONS: Everyone write imaginary events. Write in the style of a famous person. Write in the style of figures from literature or history, or other relevant subject.

SOURCE: Kerys Murrell

AUCTION

AIMS:	Self-awareness, communication skills.
MATERIALS:	Flipchart or whiteboard.
PROCEDURE:	1. The leader explains that each group member has a fixed amount of money to spend in an auction.

2. There are only ten items which may be purchased during the auction, these are (to be written on the flipchart or whiteboard):

   - A good marriage
   - Loyal friends
   - A comfortable home
   - A secure job
   - Good health
   - A high income
   - A good education
   - Children
   - Loving parents
   - Being happy

3. The leader then conducts an auction taking each 'lot' in turn, and inviting 'bids'. The item will be sold to the highest bidder. Items may be shared.
4. After each successful 'bid' the buyer must justify their choice to the rest of the group.
5. At the end of the auction, buyers sit in a circle and discuss the merits of each purchase.

VARIATIONS: Ask buyers to arrange the list in order of importance. Choose other 'lists', such as, the Ten Commandments. Use subjects within the curriculum.

SOURCE: John Norris

BACK TO BACK

AIMS: Communication, pair-work, quick thinking and memory.

MATERIALS: Pen and paper for each pair.

PROCEDURE:
1. The leader asks people to get into pairs.
2. Each member of the pair takes either the letter A or B.
3. The leader instructs the pairs to sit on the floor back to back.
4. All the 'As' remain seated on the floor and are given a blank sheet of paper and a pen.
5. The whole class is told that the 'Bs' are going to be given the name of an object which, on returning to their partner they will describe in detail. Their partner will then attempt to draw the object.
6. All the 'Bs' are given the same object to describe and are instructed that under no circumstances are they to, a) name the object or, b) use any descriptions other than direction, e.g. left, right, up, down, etc.
7. The 'Bs' return to position and the whole group begins the activity at the same time.
8. The winning pair are the pair who complete the drawing first and are successful in identifying the object based on this description.

VARIATIONS: A draws the route from their house to school and includes all the streets and landmarks. B attempts to replicate this based on A's description.

SOURCE: John Norris

BREAK MY CODE

Individuality, communication, understanding, imagination.

MATERIALS: Pens and paper. Extracts from a book (optional).

PROCEDURE:
1. Each participant is told that they will be creating a code based on the alphabet that needs to be logical, but challenging.
2. Each participant is given a pen and paper and is allowed 5 minutes planning time to create a code, e.g. vowels are replaced by numbers.
3. Participants are given a book extract which they must copy out in their own code.
4. Group members return to the 'whole group' situation and the leader collects all extracts then redistributes them so that each member is trying to crack someone else's code.

VARIATIONS: Could be used as a revision technique in English to achieve better understanding of a famous extract. Could give out 'unseen' extracts so that the task is more challenging. Could begin certain words with a symbol to replace that part of the word, e.g. ★fish = starfish.

SOURCE: John Norris

BUTTERFLIES

AIMS: To break barriers between people so that they gain in confidence and self-awareness.

MATERIALS: Pens and paper.

PROCEDURE:
1. The leader will ask participants to talk about the use of touch and how often they think people touch each other in the course of a day.
2. Group members get into pairs.
3. The leader talks the pairs through the following sequence and at the end asks them to discuss how they felt at each barrier, first they should discuss it with their partner and then with the whole group. (Participants are told they can stop at any barrier if they don't feel comfortable.)

   Barrier One
   Please face your partner and talk to them, one at a time for one minute. Keep facing your partner, don't talk and look at them for one minute.

   Barrier Two
   Look at your partner for one minute, don't talk but touch them on the hand lightly, a butterfly touch, once or twice during the minute.

   Barrier Three
   Look at your partner, don't talk and remain in contact with them for half a minute, i.e. touch feet or touch hands.

   Barrier Four
   One of the pairs closes their eyes, the other one touches their face briefly. At the same time telling them something positive about themselves. For example, "You are a good listener. I think anyone could talk to you".

4. The partners and then the group discuss the barriers and how difficult it is to cross them.

VARIATIONS: There are not really any except to change the timing.

SOURCE: Pauline Maskell

THE DISPLAY CABINET

AIMS: Group work, confidence-building, communication, understanding.

MATERIALS: A large selection of objects associated with one particular theme, e.g. 40 artifacts from World War II laid out on a table. Pen and paper.

PROCEDURE:
1. Explain to the group that they will be working in groups of 3 to create a 'display cabinet' suitable for a museum.
2. Each group is given pens and paper and are told that they must pick 3 items from the selection which they feel would best illustrate the theme. Each group is also told that they will be producing a 3 sentence paragraph about each item.
3. Once individual groups have selected and written their paragraphs, the whole group returns to their seats.
4. In turn, each group displays their three items, explains why they thought them to be important, and reads out their paragraphs.

VARIATIONS: Give each group a table on which to display the items and coloured paper so that appropriate labels can be made. The whole group can then walk around the 'Museum'. Cross curriculum themes, e.g. Christian artefacts (RE). The Museum of Japan (Geography), Museum of Healthy Food (Technology). Groups ask questions about each item within their display.

SOURCE: John Norris

FANTASY

AIMS: To encourage participants to relax and use their creative imaginations to help increase self-esteem.

MATERIALS: A comfortable darkened room, a tape recorder, soothing instrumental background music to the taste of the group, coloured pens, large sheets of paper.

PROCEDURE: The facilitator needs to practise this beforehand but does not need any special training, only confidence and a voice that is calm and relaxing. The facilitator will:

1. Ask the participants to make themselves comfortable and suggest that they can sit or lie down if they wish. (Cushions and mattresses are not needed but a safe place is necessary. Alternatively, they can sit in a chair.)
2. Ask them to close their eyes and concentrate on the voice of the facilitator.
3. Ask them to concentrate on their breathing.
4. Tell them several times that they have this time just for themselves and that at this time no one will ask them to do anything.
5. Ask them to imagine a large white, blank sheet of paper.
6. Suggest that they think of a beautiful place to which they really enjoyed going and of which they have happy memories.
7. Suggest that they recall how they felt when they were there.
8. Ask them to concentrate particularly on that memory so that they are able to describe what they saw afterwards.
9. Ask them to remember how they felt. Ask them to think of something which would remind them of this happy time and place on another occasion.
10. The facilitator will leave them with their thoughts for a few minutes whilst the background music is still running. (If people find concentration difficult the facilitator just needs to keep up the soothing statements repeating them several times calmly.) The facilitator will then ask them to open their eyes, slowly stretch and wake up, then ask them to draw what they saw and to share their experiences and their pictures with a partner.

VARIATIONS: No drawings, just discussion between partners. The facilitator can introduce into the instructions that group members should bring in a souvenir to help them to remember their pleasant memory.

SOURCE: Pauline Maskell

THE FEELINGS GAME

AIMS: To allow people to express their feelings.

MATERIALS: Pencil and paper.

PROCEDURE:
1. The leader will ask the group members to work alone at first and to make a list of ten feelings which they experience most often.
2. Then with the help of a partner, group members will be asked to write a sentence to accompany each feeling. (e.g. I feel hurt because you did not tell me you were leaving without me.)
3. The leader will ask them to make these statements with genuine feeling so that their partner can really believe them, in other words they will be asked to role-play the statements.
4. Partners will discuss how easy or hard they find it to show their feelings normally and discuss them with others.

VARIATIONS: Make a list of feelings for specific situations, e.g. when you are angry, weepy, sick, resentful, guilty, depressed, when you have suffered loss, or are alone.

SOURCE: Pauline Maskell

FIST AND FLAT

AIMS: To explore and experience aspects of assertiveness and win–win relationships.

MATERIALS: None.

PROCEDURE: Using a device similar to the traditional 'Stone, Paper, Scissors' game, pairs of participants find the consequences of adopting a win–lose or win–win strategy for scoring points. In pairs (A and B), and seated either side of a table, participants simultaneously move their forearms up and down with fists clenched, at the end of the third 'down' they show either a clenched 'fist' or an open palm ('flat'). They score points according to the resulting combination:

A	B	A	B
Fist	Flat	4	0
Flat	Flat	3	3
Fist	Fist	0	0
Flat	Fist	0	4

I usually get them to play ten rounds and keep a cumulative score, after some discussion they can then be invited to talk to their partner and play another ten. Numerous issues can emerge, e.g. trust, negotiation, win–win relationships, assertiveness and parallels can be drawn with everyday situations.

SOURCE: Jackie Harvey

HANDIWORK

AIMS: Self-esteem, trust, promoting positive communication. Celebration.

MATERIALS: Paper, pens, cellotape or pins.

PROCEDURE:
1. Each person draws an outline of their hand on a piece of A4 paper, and gets someone to stick it on their back.
2. Participants move around the room, writing positive messages to each person on their hand drawings. Essential Rule: no sarcastic statements or insults allowed.

VARIATIONS: Use hearts for Valentine's Day, eggs for Easter and so on. Use foreign languages. Participants write positive messages to themselves.

NOTES: No one is too old or too young for this game as long as they can read and write. Colleagues have been known to display their hands in their office afterwards. You could frame it. Ask people if it is as easy to write positive statements about themselves. If not (and that's usually the case), explore the reasons why. A big question for all of us!

SOURCE: Donna Brandes
John Norris

I AM, I WAS, I WANT TO BE

AIMS: Communication, trust.

MATERIALS: Pieces of paper, pens.

PROCEDURE:
1. The players are divided into groups of 4 or 5.
2. Each participant writes down three adjectives to describe:
   a) how they are feeling;
   b) how they have felt about themselves in the past;
   c) how they would like to be in the future.
3. The pieces of paper are collected by one member of each group, folded in half, and then shuffled.
4. Each group member then takes one of the pieces of paper and attempts to guess who wrote the words.
5. At the end of the session each group member 'owns up' and explains to the rest of the group their reasons for using the words.

VARIATIONS: Use other categories, e.g. favourite songs, books, plays, TV programs, events, etc. Play the game in a foreign language.

SOURCE: John Norris

IMAGINARY PLACES

AIMS: Relaxation, personal awareness, creative thinking, listening.

MATERIALS: None.

PROCEDURE: This activity is a variation of **Fantasy [p.76]**. One person thinks of a place, e.g. in the ocean, in a town, etc. The group asks questions to work out where the person is, to which they are only allowed to answer "Yes" or "No".

VARIATIONS: The class closes their eyes while one person takes the group to a special place. Students share their imaginary places with one another.

SOURCE: Harvey Agricultural Senior High School

LISTENING LESSONS

Here are some easy-to-use techniques for reinforcing listening skills. They can be used when discussing any subject.

CONCH

Choose an object to use as a conch (a felt pen, small box, ruler, ball, etc) – the idea is taken from *Lord of the Flies*. Explain that a person can speak only when they are holding the conch. When a speaker has finished, they pass the conch directly to the next person who wants to speak. This usually brings order to a discussion. It's amazing how much authority an inanimate object can have.

TOKENISM

Give everyone 3 tokens (buttons, counters, pieces of card, etc). Each time a person makes a contribution to the discussion they surrender a token, putting it in a box in the middle of the circle. The number of tokens per person can vary according to the size of the group. This simple device starts to equalise participation, by limiting the garrulous and encouraging the shy.

SUM UP AND SPEAK UP

When a person wants to contribute to a discussion, they must first sum up what the previous speaker said and then give their own opinion. Every so often the teacher shouts, "Sum up and speak up", whereupon someone volunteers to sum up the main points of the discussion so far, drawing applause from the whole group.

RANDOMISER

The teacher prepares two identical sets of cards (playing cards or handmade numbered cards). One set is distributed to the class, one per person. The other is retained by the teacher, shuffled publically and 'cut' by a pupil. The teacher turns over the top card revealing which member of the class is to speak first. When the first speaker is finished, the next card is turned over. The second person must sum up the first speaker and then make their own contribution, and so on. Though tough, this process is usually accepted as fair. It works particularly well when a sequence of ideas is being created or recalled – such as steps in an experiment, historical events, developments in a story, etc. It is also good for opening discussion of sensitive issues (for example, in RE or PSE) when pupils might be reluctant to volunteer to speak. 'Used' cards should be returned to the bottom of the pack. Every now and then the teacher should reshuffle the pack, just to keep everyone on their toes.

DEBRIEF

Asking questions about successes and difficulties, and discussing when in school it might be important for the students and the teacher to use active listening. Listening has such a positive impact on self-esteem. Also, it is the feature of group life most generally required for non-didactic approaches to work. Listening is the basis of class 'Ground Rules', and of discussion, negotiation, conflict resolution, peer assessment, decision-making and the tutoring process.

APPLICATIONS: In any subject – the topics chosen to talk about could be relevant to the syllabus. Essential as a foundation for PSE and tutorial work. Most arguments are resolved by first asking pupils to listen to each other and feed back to each other what they have said. At an advanced level the exercise could be conducted in a foreign language.

This exercise alone will not create a listening class. This will only happen if active listening is consistently expected of the students and modelled by the teacher.

SOURCE: Paul Ginnis

POOR JOHN

AIMS: A powerful activity for combatting the put down habit. Gets students to understand and explore the negative effects of 'put downs'.

MATERIALS: The Poor John story (there are enough put downs in the story for a class of 30), a large cartoon drawing (on A2 or larger) of a rather sad and neglected boy – Poor John.

The Poor John Story

The alarm goes off. John turns over for 'Just one more minute' in his nice warm bed. All of a sudden his mum's angry voice comes blasting up the stairs. "John! … John! … " She screams. "Get up you lazy good for nothing or you'll be late for school."

He looks at his pile of clothes in the corner. 'I suppose I'll have to put them on again', he thinks to himself … 'but they're going to laugh at me. They are always laughing at me'. Half dressed he rushes to the bathroom to find it locked. His sister ignores his pleas to hurry up and tells him to "GET LOST!" At last he gets in and scrubs and polishes for all he is worth.

At the breakfast table he pours himself a bowl of his favourite cereal only to find that his sister has used all the milk. John decides not to say anything and goes without his breakfast for another day.

His father comes down, takes one look at his son and scowls. "For crying out loud John. Look at the state of you. If you don't buck your ideas up you'll end up a tramp."

On his way to school he meets up with Mike and tries to talk about last night's TV. Rachel joins them and as soon as she does, Mike ignores John and talks to Rachel for the rest of the journey. 'Nobody likes me', he thinks as he walks behind them.

In school, John needs the teacher's help with his Maths. As he approaches the desk, he hears the whisper "Dumb John" ripple round the class.

It is break time. He goes into the toilets and finds everyone else rushing out, pointing at him and laughing. "STIG … STIG … " ❶ they shout. He waits until they are gone, goes in, and sees an insulting poem about him written on the toilet wall but he cannot rub it off no matter how hard he tries. He turns round and looks in the mirror. "Why don't they leave me alone?" He says out loud to his reflection.

"All I want them to do is leave me alone." In the playground he sits by himself in the corner. A group of older boys come over, steal his bag and throw it around between them. He yells out for them to stop but they just laugh. The bag falls to the floor spilling the contents into the dirt. The homework he spent hours on is ruined.

As he bends down to pick up his books one of the boys kicks him hard. He falls over and gets mud on his trousers. "Never mind", says the boy, "Nobody will notice any difference!"

He goes to PE. While changing, one of the boys steals his trainer and throws it in the shower. This makes him late for the lesson. The PE teacher picks him out. "Late again, John?" He says shaking his head. "You're always late. Detention for you, boy. Perhaps that will teach you to arrive on time!"

"But sir ... but sir ..." John tries to explain, but the teacher waves him away. The rest of the boys snigger. Their plan had worked. The boys line up. The captains are choosing sides. John is the last to be picked for the team. "We'd rather do without him, sir ... " "So would I." Said the teacher shaking his head ... and when he misses an easy shot, someone shouts, "What did we have to have him on our side for?"

Back in class, his art teacher tells him to start his picture again because his previous effort was 'a waste of paper'. Peter refuses to lend him a paint brush, saying he doesn't want his equipment to stink.

John spends hours on his design. While he is sharpening a pencil one of the other boys draws all over his work and then watches with glee as a tear forms in John's eye. "He's nearly crying. Look, everyone, he's nearly crying", shouts the boy.

The teacher wonders what all the fuss is about. He picks John out without realising what has happened. "Not you again, John. There's always something wrong with you!"

In the discussion at the end of the session, it's John's turn to speak but Peter interrupts.

In the Humanities lesson, the boys flick paper at him and try to kick him under the table.

In the English lesson, John makes a mistake when reading. The girls laugh and snigger. John thinks to himself, 'If only I could read, everything would be okay'. At last it's the end of the day and he walks home alone. He shows his mum the ash tray he made in pottery class. "Look at that, mum," he says, "I made it for you". But his mum tells him she only wants glass ones in the house. She throws it in the bin.

John struggles with his homework and asks Dad for help. "Can't you do anything on your own?" His dad says as he switches on the TV and turns up the volume … "You're useless boy. Useless!"

John is told to make the sandwiches for tea because everyone is busy. When he complains that it's always him who has to do the jobs and not his sister, his mother tells him that she is the intelligent one and needs the time to study. John's been in his bedroom for two hours and decides to go out for a walk. When the others see him coming they run away.

He walks the streets on his own, hands in his pockets, wondering what will happen to him tomorrow. At last he's home. No one notices him come in. They are too busy watching TV.

He goes to his room, says "Goodnight" but gets no reply. He sets the alarm and climbs into his bed. At least when he's asleep no one can put him down.

❶ 'STIG' is a slang word for tramp, hobo.

PROCEDURE:
1. Within the circle, establish what the put downs are.
2. Introduce Poor John to the class by showing them the cartoon drawing.
3. The leader then explains, "You are going to hear the story of Poor John. His life is very sad because wherever he goes and whatever he does, he is put down from morning till night. His family do it, his class do it and sometimes even his teachers get involved. As you listen to the story, everytime you think you hear Poor John being put down, I want you to tear a piece off Poor John, keep it safe, hold it still, and pass his picture on to the next person. Some of the put downs will be very easy to identify. Some will be tricky. Please remember that the picture has to go all the way around the group."
4. The leader or a volunteer reads the story.
5. As the put downs are identified, the picture is torn and passed around.
6. Debrief the activity, e.g. What has happened to Poor John? (he has been torn to bits). How did this happen? What has the day been like for John? How does John feel about himself? What might happen to John if this goes on day after day, week after week? Who is doing this to John? Are the people in John's life aware of what's happening to him? etc.

Part Two (allow 30 minutes)
7. A volunteer reads the story again, but this time when any particular put down is read, the person holding that piece of Poor John says, as simply as possible, (and with help if required), what could have been done to avoid the put down. When this is clear

the student symbolically places their piece of Poor John in the centre of the circle and lays that part of his day to rest.

8. It is at this stage that the teacher can move if they want from the third party story of 'Poor John' to the first party experiences of the class. (Please be aware that some students may already be doing this and transferring parts of Poor John's experiences to themselves or others.)

9. Using the opportunities that will arise and their judgement, the leader can ask questions of the group, e.g. Has this sort of put down ever happened to anyone in this class? Has anyone been called hurtful names, been kicked, been ignored, been picked out because they are not very good at something, or, had their work destroyed? If so, What does it feel like? The discussion can then be positively centred on the group's feelings and experiences. I call this part of the activity 'going live' and although it brings with it certain risks, it is usually an important step for the group to take, perhaps leading on to other related activities like a discussion of skills needed to handle insulting behaviour, or issues relating to self-esteem. Finally the leader might ask, What is self-esteem and how can we help each other to feel good about ourselves?

NOTES: The idea for Poor John came originally from an activity in *Your Choice* by Shay McConnon published by Nelson but has been further developed as this story and experiential activity by Harry Pearce. It has been used mainly with year 7 and 8 students as part of a whole school course on developing classroom rules and skills.

SOURCE: Harry Pearce

A QUESTION OF WORDS

AIMS: To identify the language of self-esteem, because the way you express yourself affects how you feel about yourself.

MATERIALS: Coloured pens, large sheets of paper, flipchart or whiteboard.

PROCEDURE:
1. The leader should ask participants to work in groups of three or four.
2. Each group needs a selection of coloured pens and a large sheet of paper.
3. The leader reads out a series of situations in turn:

   - A friend asks you out for the evening but you don't want to go
   - You are accused of doing something you did not do
   - You are unable to meet a deadline date
   - A close friend is really upset
   - You want to explain something to someone you know but they do not seem to understand you

4. Group members write down on a large sheet of paper several possible responses they might make, working together to pool their ideas.
5. The leader repeats the process reading out another situation and the participants write their response in a different coloured pen.
6. Each response statement from the group as a whole is discussed and put into one of two categories as to whether they show positive self-esteem or negative self-concept (see Example).

   Example: You are asked to help organise a birthday party celebration for a friend. Your response might be "I don't think I can do that because I have never done it before, I certainly don't think I am capable of organising the food, getting the music laid on, asking everyone to come. No one would listen to me." (Negative self-concept). Or, you might say "I've never done anything on this scale before. If a few people helped me I might be able to do it." (Positive self-esteem).

RAPID MIMES

AIMS: Spatial awareness, teamwork, creativity, communication.

MATERIALS: None.

PROCEDURE:
1. Groups of 6, 7 or 8.
2. Each group needs a large space to work in.
3. The groups are told that each round will begin by the leader shouting out a word. Each group has thirty seconds to physically 'mime' the word, ensuring that each group member is engaged in the activity.
4. The leader asks the students what they thought was good and clear, and then how they could get better at mime.
5. Examples of rounds could include; a clock, a washing machine, a table, an elephant, a window, a garden, a letter from the alphabet.

VARIATIONS: Let each group decide its own mime and allow the other groups to guess what it represents. Use words in a foreign language. Use emotions.

SOURCE: John Norris

SHIPWRECK

AIMS: To develop self-esteem with group cohesion and a sense of belonging.

MATERIALS: None.

PROCEDURE: 1. The leader will ask a group of 6 people to start acting out the following story. The rest of the group will be active spectators. This means that they can offer constructive suggestions on the story and what each actor could do. In other words, they are helping to write the script. They can also, with agreement from the acting group, substitute themselves for one of the actors.

The story
Once upon a time a group of friends set out on a voyage in a small ship. Unfortunately a storm blew up and they were washed off course. They had a very rough night and at dawn found they were far away from the usual shipping lanes and close to a small island. They had very little idea where they were. The ship's radio seemed to be working, but not very well.

2. The acting group need to make a decision about how they will get to the island and what they will do when they get there. Then they will have to act out the situation making the decisions between them and with the help of the spectating group.

3. The leader will lead a discussion about group feelings at the end, when new ideas seem to be drying up.

VARIATIONS: Ask the group to collectively write their own story. Put more decision-making skills into the story by making it a crisis situation, e.g. someone has to go for help, who will it be? Someone needs an operation, who will do it?

SOURCE: Pauline Maskell

SINNERS AND SAINTS

AIMS: To see situations from different perspectives.

MATERIALS: Paper and pens.

PROCEDURE:
1. The leader asks participants to work in groups of 3 or 4.
2. The leader reads out one of the following two stories as dramatically as possible:

Story one
The alarm clock does not go off so you get up late, miss breakfast, miss your bus and arrive late for your meeting. Several people talk to you but none of them seem to be in a very good mood, so you rush on. Someone asks you why you are late and someone else asks if you have finished the report which was needed for today.

Story two
You get up on time and the sun is shining through the window. You eat your cereal slowly and watch television at the same time. It is such a nice day you decide to walk to your meeting instead of getting the bus. You remember to take the report you finished last night. Everyone you talk to smiles at you. Everyone seems to have had a good weekend.

2. The leader asks participants to write down words which will explain how they are feeling in the first story.
3. The leader then reads out the second story and participants are again asked to record their feelings.
4. The leader asks the group to discuss why they felt differently about the two situations.

VARIATIONS: Participants can write their own situations and discuss their feelings. Groups can write out a situation for other groups to discuss.

SOURCE: Pauline Maskell

THOUGHT PATTERNS

AIMS: To identify self-perception, because the way you think about yourself affects the way you present yourself to others.

MATERIALS: Paper, coloured pencils or pens.

PROCEDURE: 1. The leader explains that they are going to read out a series of decision-making situations:

- You are asked suddenly to give a talk to a small group of people
- You want to end a relationship
- You are invited to a job interview and you really want the job
- You are given the opportunity of going on a course which involves your favourite hobby
- You meet someone you used to know but do not know what to say to them

2. The leader explains the following:

Each individual will need to write down what they would think and feel in each situation. Each person will then need to find a partner and share with them their thoughts and feelings in those situations. Pairs will then join to make fours and suggest alternative ways of acting, in order to show confident decision-making skills. The fours will then discuss with the whole group the differences in approach.

VARIATIONS: Ask the group to write a series of decision-making situations, put them in a bag and each small group take a situation out of the bag. (This is a much better idea as you will get situations the group can relate to.)

SOURCE: Pauline Maskell

TRADING PLACES

AIMS: To develop self-esteem by giving equal power to each member of the group.

MATERIALS: A comfortable, safe room.

PROCEDURE: 1. The leader asks participants to get themselves into groups of 4. The leader then reads the groups the following scenario:

You are walking along a cliff path home in a group after visiting friends, because it is the quickest way home. The sky darkens suddenly and it begins to rain. The wind gets up.
One person has a torch.
One person is certain they know the way because they have been along the path before. They tell everyone how to get back.
One person goes in front, then disappears from view.
One person gets really frightened of the dark.

2. The leader asks each group to:

a)   assign these roles to group members
b)   run the story through and to finish off the scene
c)   change roles and run through it again
d)   discuss how they felt throughout the scene
e)   discuss whether they felt anyone was taking charge
f)   report how they felt about their own first role
g)   discuss their ability to fit themselves into their role and to think about what other people were thinking and feeling
h)   think whether they behaved differently in different roles

VARIATIONS: Use a different story. Ask the groups to write their own story. Use a scene from a film or television program.

SOURCE: Pauline Maskell

Section Two
Learning Games

ANAGRAM CHARADES

AIMS:	Creativity, lateral thinking, organisation, teamwork, synergy.
MATERIALS:	Small squares of paper on each of which a number and the letter of a word has been written, e.g. if the first word to be dramatised is 'earthquake' each letter of the word is written on a separate slip of paper together with the number 1. Letters of the next word bear the numeral 2, etc.
NOTES:	It is important to complete all instructions before the players select slips and separate into word groups. From that point on they proceed without interruption. The leader should circulate among the groups in case they are having trouble figuring out what the word is and to make sure they do not spend too much time deciding upon a story, rather than moving into trying out ideas.
PROCEDURE:	1. The group is assembled to hear the instructions. The area in which the game is played should permit groups to separate and rehearse without interfering with each other. Ideally there should be a few separate rooms in which this can be done. The group is also advised at the start of the game that they will have___minutes to prepare their dramatisation. At the end of that time they will reassemble and each group presents its scenes to the other groups in turn. Allow 15–30 minutes to prepare, depending on number and type of groups and time available.

2. The slips of paper are placed in a hat in the centre of the room, the leader being careful to ensure they are mixed up.

3. Each player selects a slip and joins other players with the same numbered slip. (Left over slips are distributed to the numbered groups by the leader. Conversely, if there are too few slips, the extra players can be assigned to groups.)

4. As soon as players find their group, they attempt to unscramble their word. Once the word is known to the group they retire and improvise a charade to dramatise the word. Words used for this game should consist of two syllables. Each syllable should have dramatic potential, e.g. earthquake, rainfall, Shakespeare, warfare, etc.

Groups are encouraged to develop scenes based upon the individual syllables and the word as a whole. They may use tableau (acting a scene in rehearsal, bringing it to a peak and freezing at that point into a tableau, presenting only the tableau to the audience), pantomime, or merely dramatisation with words and props. Props can be human – like a player portraying an inanimate object.

The key to dramatic presentation is to ensure that each scene, while improvised and rehearsed only briefly, has a beginning, a middle and an end. It should tell a story – hang together. The audience is asked not to guess what the word is until all the scenes have been performed.

If possible, each group should include a person who has previously participated in this type of informal charade, and thus, may provide limited direction. Their efforts should be aimed at ensuring that each member of the group has an opportunity to share in creating the story and selecting their own role for each scene, rather than having it foisted upon them by an over eager player who is full of ideas and takes up the reigns.

VARIATIONS: English Charades. American Charades. Tag Charades.

97

BROKEN INFORMATION

AIMS: Cooperation, listening, thinking.

MATERIALS: Cards. Flipchart or whiteboard

PROCEDURE:
1. Best played with participants in a circle, but not impossible in conventional seating arrangements.
2. The leader writes the following coded message on the board:

79 13 4 5 6 9
1 5 7 8 2 6 7 10 11 10 12 10 9 3

3. The leader hands each person or pair one of the following 13 clues written out on cards.

$O \times E = 10$
$N < 10$
$3 \times D = 12$
$O + E = S$
$Y - O = R$
$YD = U - R$
$3D = L$
$2 \times P = N + I$
$O + Y = E$
$3Y + 2 = B$
$Y^2 = T$
$2 \times Y = N$
$3 \times O = N$

4. The leader explains that the message on the board can be solved as a group by using all the clues. Everyone must stay in their seat – except for one person who is nominated 'writer' and can use the board. Everyone keeps their own clue. People share their clues and ideas by talking.

VARIATIONS: The introduction of a time limit creates a sense of urgency.

SOURCE: Paul Ginnis

THE BULLYING BOWL

AIMS: Anti-bullying, teasing, sarcasm. Discussion starter.

MATERIALS: None.

PROCEDURE:
1. Anonymously, pupils must write down on a piece of paper, one form of bullying.
2. Collect all the pieces of paper and put them in a bowl.
3. Pick one out, and use it as a topic for a value continuum, or for a discussion or round.
4. Discussion.
5. Pick new ones out of the bowl.

VARIATIONS: Have 4 people on a panel, and pupils submit questions 'from the floor'.

NOTE: A value continuum can be played out against a wall of the class-room. One corner of the room is designated for the people of one extreme point of view and the next corner for the people of the opposite extreme view. Each person is then invited to place themselves, according to their opinion or practice regarding the topic, somewhere along the imaginary scale of degrees, on or between the two extremes. If two or more people wish to share the same point they can queue or sit outwards from the wall.

SOURCE: Donna Brandes
John Norris

CIRCLES

AIMS: Trust, communication, group integration.

MATERIALS: Poster paper, coloured pens.

PROCEDURE:
1. All members of the group are given poster paper and coloured pens.
2. The leader instructs the group to write their name, or draw themselves, in the centre of the paper.
3. The group is then asked to think of people who are important to them, and to place them individualy around the paper according to how close they are to the person at this moment in time, i.e. a friend who has become more distant recently might be placed on the edge of the paper.
4. The names of the people chosen should be circled.
5. An arrow can be placed close to each circle, pointing inwards or outwards, to indicate whether this person has become more or less close in recent times.
6. The group can be asked to work in smaller groups, whereby each participant can explain the reasons for their choices.

VARIATIONS: None.

SOURCE: John Norris

CONNECTIONS

AIMS: Communication, linking, teamwork.

MATERIALS: Pre-prepared pieces of paper carrying the names of events, people or dates (depending on the subject content of the activity) and several balls of string, wool or cotton.

PROCEDURE:
1. The group leader asks for a number of volunteers (8–12).
2. The volunteers stand spaced well apart around the room.
3. Each volunteer is given a piece of paper.
4. The group leader gives the ball of string to any of the volunteers, and asks that they tie themselves around the waist.
5. They may then join themselves to another member of the group if they can explain a connection to the rest of the class. They then move back to their original position, with the new person holding the string.
6. Each new person then takes the string and begins the activity anew.
7. It is permissible to re-connect with the same person, but a new connection has to be given.
8. The activity ends after a suitable time, or number of connections.

VARIATIONS: (History) Use historical events, people, dates. (Geography) Use places, cities, rivers, goods, services, etc. (Science) Use scientific concepts, pressure, gravity, light, mass, names of scientists, etc. (Social Science) Use studies and concepts, e.g. political institutions and groups. (Languages) When two people connect they use both of their words, together, to make a sentence.

SOURCE: John Norris

FAMILY CHAOS

AIMS: Fun, mixing, releasing energy, listening, team-building.

MATERIALS: Pre-prepared bits of paper, with the names of different animal family members written on them – 4 to a family, e.g. Mummy Monkey, Daddy Monkey, Teenage Monkey and Baby Monkey; Daddy Penguin, Mummy Penguin, Teenage Penguin and Baby Penguin, and so on depending on the size of the group.

PROCEDURE:
1. The leader gives out bits of paper.
2. People mill around and randomly swap their pieces of paper as quickly as possible.
3. When the leader shouts "Families", the members of each family have to find each other, by shouting "monkeys" or "penguins", etc.
4. When a family has all 4 members together, they sit down on a chair with Daddy on the bottom, then Mummy, then Teenager, and finally, Baby.
5. The last family to sit in their pile must immediately have an argument about any topic related to their lifestyle. (e.g. Penguins could argue about whose turn it is to do the fishing)

VARIATIONS: Families find each other using only animal noises. Families find each other in complete silence, or using a foreign language or accent. Use famous families, e.g. The Royal Family.

NOTES: This is a great game for releasing energy and mixing people up. It can also be used as a precursor for discussion work on family issues and gender roles.

SOURCE: Donna Brandes
John Norris
[A variation of Freud – see Gamesters' Handbook 2 page 61]

GETTING TO KNOW YOU

AIMS:	Group introduction, get to know each other, sharing.
MATERIALS:	None.
PROCEDURE:	1. Think of one thing you would like to tell other group members about yourself, e.g. favourite hobby, where you work, something about your family, etc.
	2. Stand up and move around the room, shaking hands with everyone and using this sentence "Hello, I'm … and I … " Say the same sentence to each group member and let them reply to you.
	3. Sit down when you have spoken to everyone.
VARIATIONS:	Give the group a certain topic to discuss, e.g. something in the news. Give the group a question to ask, e.g. "Where were you born? Would you like to live there all your life?" Give them sentence stems, e.g. "one thing I would really like to know about you is … " or something more controversial, e.g. "Media photographers should have to ask for permission to shoot pictures."
SOURCE:	Pat Havell

GROUPS GALORE

Teachers often ask what kinds of groups work best. There are many options but they all serve different purposes. Each is appropriate to particular circumstances.

Random Groups – created by sticking a pin in the register, or by numbering round the class, or by pulling names out of a hat, or by asking the class to stand in a line according to age order, then dividing the line into chunks.

Friendship Groups – people get together with their friends.

Interest Groups – people come together because they want to work on the same topic or use the same approach.

Skill Based Groups – people with a particular skill or strength form a group, e.g. all the actors, all the readers, all the artists, all the orators.

Learning Style Groups – people form groups according to their preferred learning style, e.g. discussion, trial and error, reading, structured exercises, presentation by the teacher.

Mixed-Skill Groups – each group has members with different and complementary skills, e.g. an organiser, a confident speaker, a fast reader, a motivator, a lateral thinker.

Peer Support Groups – people with self-confessed ability in a particular task get together with those with self-confessed weakness, with the intention of offering support. Given a different task, the tables may be turned.

As time goes on it is important to talk with pupils about the pros and cons of different types or groups. Before long they will be able to make the decisions themselves, and spare the teacher the headache!

SOURCE: Paul Ginnis

GUESS WHERE (YEAH YEAH)

AIMS: Sensory development, trust, memory.

MATERIALS: Blindfolds.

PROCEDURE: **1.** In pairs students move around the school or play area.

             2. Person A is blindfolded and kept out of harm's way by person B.

             3. Once a part of the school, play area, etc. has been located by person B, person A has to use their senses to work out where they are.

             4. Person B can give A clues, e.g. "Focus on what you can smell", if they are near the canteen.

SOURCE: Harvey Agricultural Senior High School

              [A variation of Trust Walk – see Gamesters' Handbook S25]

105

HOW ARE YOU FEELING TODAY?

AIMS: Reflection, communication skills, working with others.

MATERIALS: Flipchart or whiteboard.

PROCEDURE:
1. The leader explains to the group that the four corners of the room will be used for this activity, numbered 1–4. These four numbers are written on the board.
2. The leader writes down four adjectives under these headings, e.g. sad, happy, optimistic, tired.
3. Group members choose the category which most closely describes how they are feeling today.
4. They then move to the appropriate corner of the room and sit in a circle.
5. When everyone is ready, each person takes a turn saying, "I am feeling … because … "
6. When completed, the leader writes another four adjectives on the board.

VARIATIONS: Adjectives and speech in a foreign language.

NOTES: This is an activity best used with a group in which trust has already been established.

SOURCE: John Norris

MASTERMIND

AIMS: Rapid thinking, knowledge, working with others.

MATERIALS: Paper, pens, flipchart or whiteboard.

PROCEDURE:
1. Groups of 4 or 5.
2. Leader writes ten categories, as a vertical line, on the board, e.g. famous people, motor cars, countries, rivers, pop groups, etc.
3. One person in each group copies the chart.
4. The leader chooses a letter, and writes it at the top of one of the columns.
5. Groups race to find an example of each category beginning with the appropriate letter. The first group to finish shouts "stop", at which point all groups must stop.
6. The game can continue for as long as you wish.
7. Groups score one point for every correct example, or two points for any correct example that was not given by any other group. The scores are totalled at the end of the activity.

VARIATIONS: All categories could be subject related or based on a particular theme. Group size can vary. The first group to finish could choose the next letter.

NOTES: This activity can be used as a revision exercise for knowledge based subjects.

SOURCE: Helen Norris

MYSTERY BOXES

AIMS: To get to know each other, communication.

MATERIALS: In advance of the activity, the group is asked to bring in a box, which contains five items that have significance to them, e.g. a photograph of a relative, a timetable for a sports club, a postcard, etc.

PROCEDURE:
1. Each member of the group places their box in centre of the room.
2. The leader mixes the boxes up.
3. Each person is given a box at random. They are asked to open it and examine the objects.
4. Each person must then guess whose box they have, explaining their reasons for the guess to the rest of the group.
5. At the end of the round, establish how many choices were correct.
6. Each member can then explain the significance of their choice of objects.

VARIATIONS: Use photographs, which could then form part of a collage or wall display. Use less items.

NOTES: This is a particularly good activity for younger students at the start of a course, or project.

SOURCE: Helen Norris

ONE WORD AT A TIME

AIMS: Cooperation, listening, language development, creativity.

MATERIALS: None.

PROCEDURE: 1. Players sit in a circle.
2. The idea is for the group to tell a story with each person contributing, in turn, one word at a time.

VARIATIONS: As many as the imagination of the group will allow – two or more words at a turn, phrases, sentences, etc. A bottle could be spun and players try to continue their contribution to the story for as long as the bottle is spinning.

SOURCE: John Eaton, Manjimup

PAIRS TO FOURS

AIMS: To promote cooperation, practise oral and listening skills, acquire debating and decision-making skills.

MATERIALS: None.

PROCEDURE:
1. Clear the desks and ask the group to pair off.
2. Each pair should be given a task to complete, involving the need to discuss and make decisions (e.g. a ranking exercise, choosing which mock business plan to accept, creating headings for paragraphs in a text book, deciding captions for a series of photographs, etc.)
3. As pairs finish (or after a set time) two pairs join up and each pair shares the results of their labours with the other. The four then enter into further debate in order to arrive at an agreed version which will be shared with the whole class.
4. It is important that any one of the four is able to explain and defend to the rest of the class, the decisions made by their group. The teacher might want to stipulate which of the four presents their group's conclusions, rather than have the group decide who the spokesperson is to be.
5. Debrief the process, focussing on the process of decision-making and on the varying natures of consensus, compromise and conflict resolution.

VARIATIONS: If numbers (and nerves) will stand it, the fours could move into eights and so on until a whole class decision had been reached.

SOURCE: Paul Ginnis

QUICK ON THE DRAW

AIMS: A research activity with a built-in incentive for teamwork and speed.

MATERIALS: Relevant source material. Pens and paper.

PROCEDURE:
1. Prepare a set of questions about the current topic, or project.
2. Divide the class into groups of 4.
3. Give each group the relevant source material.
4. One person from each group 'runs' to the teacher for the first question and takes it back to their group.
5. Using the source material, the group researches the answer and writes it down.
6. This is taken to the teacher by the second person who (if it is correct) is given the next question, and so on.

VARIATIONS: From years 7–12, the depth and complexity of questions can be varied to suit many different contexts. Debrief the study skills used and the ways in which students can organise collaborative learning in the future. Can be played as a race against other groups or against the clock.

SOURCE: Paul Ginnis

RESHUFFLE

AIMS: Fun, trust, memory.

MATERIALS: Large open space, blindfold.

PROCEDURE:
1. Students organise themselves into groups of at least 5 and spread out.
2. The person in the middle checks to see who is standing in what position and must then put on their blindfold. The four other people can then reshuffle positions. From their mark, the person in the middle must walk blindfolded to where they think the first person is. Be sure to establish that players will not stray further than 20 steps from the blindfolded person's starting point. Also, players must not allow the blindfolded person to walk into danger.
3. Once the player wearing the blindfold has found the first person they must guess who it is. If they are incorrect the players are allowed to reshuffle. The game ends when the player in the middle has found and identified all players correctly.

SOURCE: Harvey Agricultural Senior High School

SCRAMBLED GROUPS

AIMS: To reinforce listening skills. To reinforce the idea that everyone's opinion is valuable and practice the study skills of note-taking, summarising and presenting. Encourage pupils to work in random groups.

MATERIALS: Paper and pens, enough cards with letters A, B, C, D, E for all groups (one card for each letter).

PROCEDURE:
1. The class is divided into groups of 5 and each person is given a letter A–E.
2. Each group conducts a discussion on the current topic or project.
3. During the discussion each person makes a note of the main points raised in their group.
4. At the end of this discussion period the groups are rescrambled. All the As form a new group, all the Bs form a group and so on.
5. In these new groups, people take it in turns to report on their previous group's discussion, being careful to relay all the key points.
6. Once all the reports have been heard, the group holds a final discussion, reaching a conclusion if necessary.
7. In theory, at the end of the process any one person in the class should be able to sum up a wide range of opinion.

VARIATIONS: This exercise can be applied to any subject where discussion is appropriate. Could be used as a peer teaching model. Instead of opinions, individual's research findings could be contributed to the first group discussion and reported to the second group as above.

SOURCE: Paul Ginnis

THROW A FACE

AIMS: Concentration, creativity, mime, communication, contact.

MATERIALS: None.

PROCEDURE:
1. Players sit in a circle.
2. One player puts on a wide smile, wipes it off and 'throws' it to another player.
3. The player who catches it, displays it and then changes it to another expression, wipes this off and throws it to another player.
4. This process is continued.
5. The leader may suggest players use emotions that can be easily recognised by facial expressions – surprise, disbelief, boredom, anger, etc.

SOURCE: John Eaton, Manjimup

TOUCHING

AIMS: To heighten the sense of touch and to test memory.

MATERIALS: Blindfold. Objects that can be guessed by touch.

PROCEDURE:
1. The group leader blindfolds one volunteer from the group.
2. This player is handed the objects one by one.
3. They have 5 seconds to guess what the object is and to remember it.
4. Once all the objects have been felt, the blindfold is taken off and the player must then write down as many objects as they can remember.
5. The group leader can then reveal what the objects were and how many were guessed and remembered correctly.

VARIATIONS: Everyone is blindfolded, and objects are passed around the circle in order. Work in pairs, each brings a set of objects and partners take turns being blindfolded.

SOURCE: Amy Barton
Sarah Manly
Hinchingbrooke School

115

Section Three
School Subject Games

SOME PSYCHOLOGY GAMES pp.119–123

My Advanced Level Year 12 Psychology students had shown great interest in this book, in particular the role of games in the learning process. One afternoon, I asked them whether they would like to invent some psychology games. They were extremely enthusiastic, so we decided to brainstorm some of the psychological concepts which we had encountered in the course, thus far.

Ideas flowed from Freud, Jung, and Carl Rogers, to id, ego, superego, anxiety, depression, sub-conscious, change, and phobia. Pairs of students then began work, devising an appropriate game to illustrate a key concept.

We quickly ran out of time, so I asked whether they would complete their games for the following morning, as the publishing deadline was fast approaching. All agreed, and the next morning the games arrived. No one broke their promise.

I have decided not to submit the student games on either Oedipal conflicts or penis envy! Superb and vastly amusing as they are, I think they are deserving of a more specialised audience!

John Norris

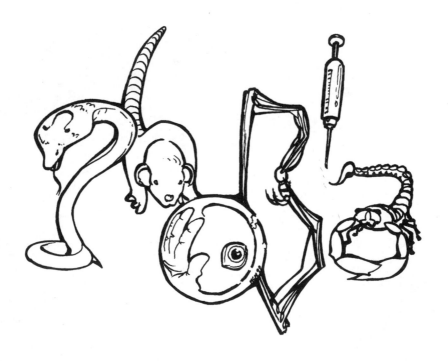

EMOTIONAL RESPONSE GAME

AIMS: Communication, interpreting behaviors, awareness of emotions.

MATERIALS: Set of cards with emotions written on each, e.g. anger, tolerance, lust, pain, etc (maximum 10–12).

PROCEDURE:
1. The group sits in a circle.
2. The cards are placed in the middle of the circle. The leader chooses one person to pick a card, then moving in a clockwise direction, each person in turn chooses a card, until all the cards are used.
3. Starting with the first person, they each act out the emotion and the rest of the group has to guess what it is.
4. The whole group then proceeds to act out a scene where each person can respond with their given emotion. The scene is decided by group agreement, e.g. one person has 'Anger', another has 'Lust', 'Lust' may say to 'Anger' "You're looking good tonight" and 'Anger' would respond with something like "Who the hell do you think you're talking to?"

SOURCE:
Jo Dowler
Mel York
Hinchingbrooke School

FEAR

AIMS: Interpersonal relationships, team-building.

MATERIALS: Paper and pens.

PROCEDURE:
1. One person leaves the room.
2. The other members of the group draw a representation of what they fear without using words.
3. The completed representations should be mixed up and placed centrally in the room.
4. The person is then brought in and has to match the picture with the person who drew it.

VARIATIONS: Any topic could be used, e.g. favourite occupations/hobbies.

SOURCE: Students of Hinchingbrooke School

PHOBIAS

AIMS: Empathy, teamwork, listening.

MATERIALS: Two sets of cards with identical phobias written on them, e.g. two cards with 'Claustrophobia' on them, etc.

PROCEDURE:
1. The group leader divides the class into two different groups (A and B) and gives each group one set of cards. Each person is given a card.
2. The people in group A take it in turns to describe how their phobia makes them feel, without saying what their phobia actually is.
3. Each person in group B has to then stand behind the person in the opposite group who they think has the same phobia card as them.

VARIATIONS: Act out the phobia. Work out a treatment plan for the phobia.

SOURCE: Dawn Fleming
Maddie Hennessy
Hinchingbrooke School

PSYCHO CHAIN MIME GAME

AIMS: Development of communication skills, creating interpersonal relationships, promote the study of behaviour, to be humorous.

MATERIALS: Paper and pens. Minimum of 10 people. Knowledge of Psychology.

PROCEDURE:
1. All participants sit in a circle, facing each other.
2. The first person thinks of a psychological concept, writes it down and places it face down in the centre of the circle.
3. The person who wrote down the concept mimes it to another person, until the thumbs up sign is given as understood. No speaking may be involved.
4. The second person then mimes to the next person in the group and so on until it reaches the last person, who then mimes to the whole group what they think the concept is.
5. Everyone writes down what they think the concept is.
6. All the answers are read out by each member in turn (maybe with accompanying explanation).
7. The original concept is revealed and everyone confers.

VARIATIONS: Psychological concepts can be changed. Number of people in group can be altered.

SOURCE: Rosalind Malone
Ellen Wright

THE ULTIMATE RESCUER

AIMS: Communication, target-setting, self-appraisal.

MATERIALS: Poster paper and coloured pens.

PROCEDURE:
1. The leader explains to the group that they are to design and draw an environment which consists of two pieces of land, separated by a large river.
2. On one side of the river is 'the land of where I am now'. On the other side is 'the land where I want to be'. The river represents an obstacle.
3. Individuals must design and draw the features of both lands.
4. In the river, individuals should draw any obstacles which stand in their way.
5. Explain that everyone is allowed to build a bridge which will enable them to reach the other side. Participants should indicate what the bridge is built from.
6. At the end of the session, work in small groups and explain the pictures.

VARIATIONS: Make the activity non-verbal.

SOURCE: John Norris

ACHILLES' HEEL

AIMS: Communication, self-awareness, recording achievement.

MATERIALS: A3 size paper which has a body outline imposed on it, pens.

PROCEDURE:
1. The leader explains to the group that each outline represents themselves.
2. Each part of the body represents an individual's strengths and weaknesses, in terms of their personality, attitudes and skills, etc.
3. On a piece of paper each person writes statements about themselves using the following guidelines:

 a) Head – mental aptitude, intelligence, etc
 b) Mouth and Ears – communication skills
 c) Eyes – vision, looking ahead, planning, etc
 d) Hands – manual dexterity, making things
 e) Shoulders – responsibility
 f) Heart – emotions
 g) Joints – flexibility of thinking
 h) Thighs – physical strength
 I) Heel – what's your Achilles' Heel?

4. Follow-up with pair or small group discussions.

VARIATIONS: Choose a partner and complete the activity on their behalf. Use giant size poster paper, with real body outlines, and pin them up around the room. Do not write your name on the poster, and let the group guess.

SOURCE: John Norris

ALPHABET RACE

AIMS: Spelling review, physical activity, fun

MATERIALS: Two sets of alphabet cards – roughly six inches square. Two tables on which the cards are spread out, face up.

PROCEDURE:
1. Players are divided into two teams and line up in columns.
2. A table is placed about 20–25 feet in front of the first player in each team.
3. The leader calls out a word.
4. In turn, players from each team run to their respective tables in an attempt to be the first person to collect the letters that spell out the word and display them in the correct order to the rest of the team, e.g. if the word is 'alphabet', eight people from each team are required to spell out the word, each runs to the table in turn and grabs the letter whose position in the word corresponds with that person's position in the line (i.e. first in line grabs 'a', second in line grabs 'l', etc). The players then form a line in front of their own remaining team members and hold up the letters, which should now spell out the word. The first team to complete the correct spelling of the word scores a point.
5. Players who have just formed a word place their letters back on the table, face up, and return to the end of their line.

NOTES: It is advisable for the leader to frequently scramble the letters on each table, since team members inevitably attempt to separate them to make it more convenient for the next player. No harm is done if some of the cards lie partly on others. Everyone coaches everyone else, confusion reigns and team spirit takes hold. This is excellent for mum, dad and the kids, if the kids are not to young. And, of course, it's good for all the in-betweens.

SOURCE: Donna Brandes

DECEPTION

AIMS: Memory, quick thinking, group work, problem-solving, persuasiveness.

MATERIALS: Pens, paper and dictionary for each individual group. The leader prepares a list of unusual words for each group.

PROCEDURE:
1. The leader divides the group into smaller groups of 3–6 members.
2. The leader gives each individual group their list of words.
3. Groups are told to write 3 definitions for each word. One must be the correct definition whilst the others must be untrue.
4. The leader informs each group that the aim of the activity is to persuade the other groups to select the wrong definition.
5. After 15 minutes groups are told to select 3 members of their group to be panel members.
6. Dictionaries are removed at this stage.
7. The leader instructs one group to give their first word to the whole group.
8. The panel of that group then read out their 3 definitions.
9. The remaining panels must then guess which they think is the real definition. This can be written down or the leader can go round each panel and write down their ideas.
10. The panel then reveals the true definition. If the opposing panels guess incorrectly, the panel that has managed to mislead them wins one point. Only a correct guess wins the other panels a point.
11. The leader then asks the second panel to read out their 3 definitions.
12. Procedure is repeated as long as required.

VARIATIONS: Allow groups to choose their own words connected to the topic being studied. Could be used as a revision technique. Could be used as an introduction to a new topic in most curriculum areas. Individual groups could be given very small time limits in which to make their choices. Could be used in particular curriculum areas, e.g. (English) Use quotes from a book and ask in which book they appear. (Religious Studies) Use to identify unusual religious artefacts. What purpose do they serve? (Mathematics) Identify correct formulae, algebraic equations, etc. (Science) Use to identify correct outcome for mixing various elements/compounds, etc.

SOURCE: John Norris

GET IN LINE

AIMS: Chronology, teamwork, quick thinking, memory.

MATERIALS: The leader needs to prepare lists of dates and famous events relevant to the theme being covered.

PROCEDURE:
1. The leader gives each member of the group a year in time, e.g. BC 364, BC 200, etc.
2. The leader instructs the group to line up in chronological order as quickly as possible explaining at which end of the line the highest year should be.
3. The leader asks group members to call out their date one by one to check that the chronological sequencing is correct.
4. The group members then return to their seats.
5. The leader then gives each group member a famous period in history. The previous procedure is repeated.
6. This part of the game can be repeated as many times as necessary.

VARIATIONS: Begin the game by asking group members to get into birth date order. Use different categories such as height, size of feet, street numbers, as the introductory theme. Use specific categories relating to curriculum areas, such as famous Kings and Queens in History, the length of major rivers in Geography, sizes of population in Geography, statistics on followers of various religions in RE, prime numbers in Maths, etc.

SOURCE: Helen and John Norris

INITIAL ANSWERS

AIMS: Learning names, mixing, memory.

MATERIALS: None.

PROCEDURE:
1. Everyone sits in a circle.
2. The leader asks a general question such as, "What is your hobby?" Each player in turn must answer in words begining with their initials, e.g. George Smith, gathering snakes, Betty Jones, baking jam rolls.
3. On failure to give an answer in five seconds the player is out.

VARIATIONS: After each player has given their answer the rest of the group guesses what their name might be.

SOURCE: Donna Brandes

LINKING LETTERS

AIMS:	Recollection, memory, quick thinking.

MATERIALS: Flipchart or whiteboard. Pen and paper for group members.

PROCEDURE:

1. The leader names a theme and lists its letters vertically on the board in capital letters.

2. The leader explains that the object of the game is to come up with words connected with the topic that will link horizontally with the original word.

3. The horizontal linking words do not necessarily have to begin with the vertical letter.

   e.g. vertical theme: FRENCH

        F r a n c e

   b e R e t

   c h E e s e

   l a N g u a g e

       C r o i s s a n t

   c H a m p a g n e

4. Having given the group an example, the leader gives them a different theme. The group then creates their own set of horizontal linking words.

VARIATIONS: Horizontal words could begin with each letter of the vertical theme – hence making the task more difficult. This exercise can be applied to most curriculum areas and could be used as a revision technique at all levels. The idea could be used as a 'guessing game' whereby the group is put into smaller groups. Each member has a related vertical theme. Each member of the group creates their horizontal words. The smaller groups pass their 'linking letters' to another group who has to guess the theme which links all the vertical words (obviously, the vertical words would not be written in capitals).

SOURCE: Helen Norris

LOVE OF MONEY

AIMS: Prioritising, building confidence, values, communication.

MATERIALS: The leader needs two identical bowls. One should be filled with coins and a few bank notes, the other should be empty. A spotlight. Pen and paper for each member of the group.

PROCEDURE:
1. The group sits in a circle.
2. The leader tells the group to pass the bowl of money around the circle. When a group member has the bowl in their possession they must say what the bowl reminds them of.
3. The same procedure is repeated using the empty bowl.
4. The leader then gives the group the task of imagining they had won 1 million pounds on the lottery. The group members should then contemplate what they would do with the money. (At this point the bowl of money can be put in the centre of the room with a spotlight highlighting its position.)
5. After 10 minutes the group complete a round whereby each member explains the way in which they spent the bulk of their winnings, giving reasons for their choices.
6. An open ended question is then asked by the leader: Is the person who wins 1 million on the lottery happier than the person who is penniless?

VARIATIONS: Focus on a particular religious teaching. For example, a wise Guru, taught that "the rich man squeezes the milk from the poor man", i.e. a poor man's work is honest whereas a rich man exploits the poor. Give the group members 'real' money to use (e.g. from the game Monopoly) so that they can actually see how much they will be spending. Obviously, their winnings may have to be less than 1 million! Ask questions about gambling, exploitation, minimum wage, 'Does wealth lead to misery?' etc.

SOURCE: Helen Norris

MAGAZINE MAYHEM

AIMS: Improvisation, imagination, sharing feelings, listening.

MATERIALS: None.

PROCEDURE: Students pair up and each chooses a character from a particular magazine, e.g. Cindy Crawford. Each person then interviews the other to find out what is happening in that person's life at the moment. The person being interviewed must role-play and relate an improvised story of their lifestyle. Selections from interviews can be shared with the entire group.

VARIATIONS: Write a story about the person's family. Draw a Family Tree.

SOURCE: Harvey Agricultural Senior High School

THE PERFECT RECIPE?

AIMS:	Communication, target-setting, self-assessment, personal development.
MATERIALS:	Pens and paper.
PROCEDURE:	1. The group should work individually or in small groups.
	2. Each individual or small group is to design a menu, which consists of a starter, main meal and dessert.
	3. The type of 'meal' to be designed will depend on the theme of the activity, e.g.

   a) a happy family
   b) a rewarding career
   c) a successful organisation
   d) good parents
   e) a system of appraisal, etc.

4. Each part of the meal can consist of various ingredients. (e.g. for 'a' above, starter might be patience and understanding, main course could be compassion with a tolerance sauce, etc.)
5. Individuals/groups are to pass their menus around, and discuss their ideas.

VARIATIONS:	Ask members of the group to request a particular menu, and allow other members to design it. Give different groups different menu's to design. Discuss what happens if you run out of particular ingredients.
SOURCE:	John Norris

POETIC LICENCE

AIMS: Word association, memory, group work, reflection, to create a haiku (Japanese poem).

MATERIALS: Each group member needs a pen and paper. Rough paper should be available for each group. Pictures/photographs relating to the theme to be displayed on the wall. Flipchart or whiteboard.

PROCEDURE:
1. The leader explains that the success of the activity is based on using the correct number of syllables for each line created.
2. The leader tells each group member that they will be creating a haiku consisting of three lines. The first line and the third line will contain 5 syllables each while the second line will contain 7 syllables.
3. The whole group is told to look at the pictures on the wall and the name of the theme, e.g. Diwali (Festival of Light in Hinduism and Sikhism).
4. The leader gives an example of how to create the first line using the pictures as a stimulus. (At this point the leader may ask the group for possible word associations or may write some key words on the flipchart or whiteboard, e.g. Deva, goddess, light, decoration, etc.)
5. Through example the leader demonstrates that each line of the haiku does not need to make sense. However it must consist of the correct number of syllables. Example of haiku for Diwali:

> Dancing round the light
> Children, music, colour, gods
> Decorated shrine
>
> Lakshmi enters house
> Singing sweetly in the night
> incense, burning pyre
>
> Masks of gold, stories
> Deva lamps light up the street
> My goddess is here

6. The leader puts the whole group into smaller groups of 3–5 members.
7. Each group member is instructed to make one verse of the haiku.
8. Groups are instructed to arrange their individual verses so that when read out, the whole haiku (for their own group) sounds well ordered.
9. The leader asks one member from each group to read out their groups own haiku.

VARIATIONS: Groups can decorate the haiku and use it for display work. Can be used to check comprehension and spelling. Could be used for specific curriculum areas, e.g. periods in History, story telling or creative writing in English, themes in French/German.

SOURCE: Helen Norris

SHAPES

AIMS: Spatial awareness, non-verbal communication.

MATERIALS: Envelopes containing the shapes illustrated below.

PROCEDURE: 1. Rule five squares, each of identical size on a piece of card or stiff paper. Rule each square into a pattern as shown below.

2. Cut the squares into the lettered shapes above.
3. Group shapes into 5 sets according to the letters.
4. Put these five sets into five envelopes and mark each with the appropriate letters. NB: Five sets will work with one group of five. Therefore make several copies for a large group.
5. The leader gives out the following instructions: Each member of the group is to have one envelope. The exercise will continue until each member has made a square. All squares must be the same size. You may pass a piece of card to another person, but you may not reach out and take one. No words may be spoken, or noises made at any point in the activity.

VARIATIONS: Instead of letters, have pictures, diagrams or drawings. Play the game blindfolded.

SOURCE: John Norris

STEREOTYPES

AIMS:	Communication, evaluation, comprehension of stereotype.
MATERIALS:	Pens and paper.
PROCEDURE:	1. The leader writes the following table on a flipchart or white-board.

Husbands Footballer, Electrician, Window Cleaner, Farm Worker, Teacher, Doctor, Dancer, Salesman

Wives Supermarket Cashier, Secretary, Nurse, Surgeon, Factory Worker, Engineer, Aerobics Instructor, Computer Programmer

Accommodation Cottage, Terraced House, Council House, Detached House, Semi-Detached House, Flat, Caravan, Converted Barn

Children Five, Four, Three, Two, One, None, Adopted, Fostered

Pets 3 Birds, Cat, 2 Cats, Dog, 2 Dogs, Rabbit, Pony, Goldfish, No Pets

Transport Mini, BMW, Ford Escort, Mercedes, Motorbike, Pushbike, No Transport

Holidays Spain, Mediterranean Cruise, Skiing, Caravan Holiday, Camping, Far Eastern Holiday, No Holiday

2. Either individually, in pairs, or small groups, the task is to create 6 'Families' using one selection from each of the seven categories.
3. Feedback session to discuss the groups results.

VARIATIONS:	Mark ✚ to show the happiest family. Mark ✖ to show the family most likely to neglect children. Mark ★ to show the one you would most like to live with. Use other categories. Play in a foreign language.
SOURCE:	John Norris

WHAT IF

AIMS:	Lateral thinking, spirited discussion of consequences.
MATERIALS:	None.
PROCEDURE:	1. The group brainstorms 'what if' questions, e.g. in Science "What if there were water on Mars?" In History "What if Henry the VIII had stayed with his first wife".
	2. Pick one topic, and discuss the 'what if' in pairs.
	3. Come up with answers to the questions.
	4. Pairs join up to make larger groups and share their answers.
VARIATIONS:	Moral dilemma – A boy asks you out, you don't like him but he's rich, what do you do? History – What if the atom bomb had not been invented? Languages – What if everyone in the world spoke the same language?
NOTES:	This game could be an adult party game, with political, religious, or personal questions.
SOURCE:	Donna Brandes
	John Norris

Section Four

Mostly just for fun

AGATHA CHRISTIE

AIMS:	Concentration, cooperation, creativity and interaction.
MATERIALS:	None.
PROCEDURE:	1. The group sits in a circle.

2. The leader starts in role as a policeman or detective: "Thank you all for staying. We will try to get this over as quickly as possible, as I know that some of you need to get away to deal with important affairs. Perhaps we could begin with a statement from whoever found the body ... "
3. Wait for the first member to volunteer and give their account. The leader in role may ask questions or challenge.
4. The other members come in with their accounts, having introduced themselves, and can either support a previous speaker or give a conflicting account. There are many options for where this game could go from here:

   a) The group could stop for discussion and plan how to take the game further
   b) The leader could arrest somebody
   c) The leader or someone else could put a spanner in the works by starting a fight or sabotage the questioning in some way
   d) The leader could bring in a witness (visitor) unknown to the group
   e) The leader could read the conclusion of an Agatha Christie novel or give copies of the book to the group to read, and then the group could discuss how these kinds of books usually end, and go away in groups to plan different endings

VARIATIONS: Continue and make the incident into a fully developed play. The crime need not be murder, it could be theft or fraud, etc.

SOURCE: Pat Havell

ALFRED

AIMS: Fun, creativity, imagination, people-watching.

MATERIALS: None.

PROCEDURE:

1. Anyone can start by looking around them and making up a story about someone they see.

2. Without making any sort of warning announcement, he/she says "See that guy over there? Well his name is Alfred, and he just got out of jail, and he's on parole. He's dining with his beautiful parole officer, who is getting more and more interested in him as a person. But she's got that hat on because she has a mushroom growing out of the top of her head. He hasn't seen it yet."

3. The next person, joining in, might say, "Yes he has, he sneaked up and watched her combing her hair by the car. He doesn't mind mushrooms."

4. After that, wherever you might go, or whatever you might be doing, someone could say, "Hey, you know Alfred? Well the reason he was in jail in the first place was for growing and selling magic mushrooms."

5. Another player could announce, "Yes, I knew that, but I bet you didn't know he made his fortune selling tinned mushroom soup."

6. You can drop the mushroom theme, and say something like, "Alfred's been calling me at all hours of the night." In other words, the idea is to keep the game going, perhaps forever, but always starting unexpectedly, in outlandish places and times.

NOTES:
(From Donna)

The first time I played Alfred, I didn't know I was playing it. I was having a Chinese meal with some British visitors, in Denmark, Western Australia, when Colin suddenly said, "See that guy over there, his name is Alfred. But that's not his wife, that's his sister-in-law. They look a bit chummy, don't they?" It took me a while to work out what he was doing. After that, he would suddenly start playing while we were surfing, or in a car, rolling among the Jarrah forests. That's the beauty of it, it's another of these portable, anywhere–anytime games, with endless variety. Of course, you can forget Alfred and start on Cynthia or Toodles.

SOURCE: Colin Cook

BECKON

AIMS: Just for fun, especially good on a camp or picnic.

MATERIALS: None, but should be played outdoors.

PROCEDURE:
1. The selection of boundaries for an area is most important to the game. A small clearly defined area in which the players can all stand is designated as the prison. It must be in a semi-exposed area so that it is neither too easy nor too difficult to flee and find a hiding place. The total area for playing should provide many hiding places, from which a player can see the prison.
2. One person is 'it' and hides their eyes, giving the other players a count of 100 or 200 (depending on the area) to find a hiding place. They count while standing at the prison.
3. The players scatter, each finding their own hiding place, making sure that the hiding place permits them to be seen from the prison if they were to reveal themselves.
4. On finishing the count, 'it' looks for the other players. When they see one, they identify them by name or by what they are wearing and state exactly where the player is hiding. The captured player then walks to the prison unaccompanied.
5. As soon as a captured player is in prison they loudly call for a 'Beckon'. This can be granted by any free player, by beckoning to the prisoner with their finger in order to be spotted by the prisoner. When a prisoner receives a beckon they can leave the prison at any time. They do not have to leave the moment they receive it. If they succeed in fleeing the prison and find another hiding place without being seen by 'it' they are free to give beckons to other players. If, however, 'it' sees them escaping and identifies them as before, they must return to prison. To escape again they must call for and receive another beckon.
6. 'It' must try to capture all the players, finding those still hidden while at the same time keeping the captured players in prison.
7. The game ends when 'it' has all the players in prison.

VARIATIONS: The game could be played with two players being 'it' if the group is very large.

SOURCE: Donna Brandes

CATS CRADLE

AIMS:	Teamwork, fun, building trust, communication skills.
MATERIALS:	String, tables, blindfolds, stopwatch.

PROCEDURE:

1. Tie the string randomly between the table legs, to form a cats cradle.
2. Divide the group into pairs, it is best if the pairs do not know each other.
3. Blindfold one of the pair. The other person is known as 'Leader'.
4. 'Leader' will instruct their blindfolded partner verbally how to cross the cats cradle without touching the string.
5. If they touch the string, the pair have to start again.
6. Repeat the exercise with the roles reversed.

VARIATIONS: Use a stopwatch to time the pairs. Play with three people, but tie two of their legs together – e.g. three legged.

SOURCE: Joanna Barnes
Lauren Roberts
Katherine Sewell
Hinchingbrooke School

DETECTIVE

AIMS: Problem-solving, imagination, logical thinking.

MATERIALS: A wallet, handbag or similar, containing pieces of personal information, e.g. credit cards, receipts, membership cards, bank notes, etc.

PROCEDURE:
1. Divide participants into small groups.
2. Place the bag/wallet, etc. in the centre of the room, and allow each group to inspect the contents.
3. Explain to the group that they have to construct a police profile of the missing person, which must include their personal details and habits.
4. Each group presents its ideas.

VARIATIONS: The profile could be written in a foreign language. The clues could be pieces of historical evidence, indicating a famous character.

SOURCE: John Norris

ELEPHANT AND GIRAFFE

AIMS: Fun, concentration, coordination.

MATERIALS: None

PROCEDURE:
1. Players stand in a circle, close enough to reach their neighbours without straining.
2. One player is chosen to be 'it' and stands inside the circle.
3. 'It', without taking a long time, points at a player standing in the circle and says either "elephant" or "giraffe".
4. If 'it' says "elephant", the player pointed at places both their fists in front of their nose to simulate a trunk, while the players on their immediate right and left simultaneously cup their nearest hand behind the middle player's ears.
5. If 'it' says "giraffe", the player pointed at raises both arms directly above their head while their immediate neighbours shoot their hands straight in front of them. (The hand should be at right angles to the body of the middle player, parallel to the floor. Do not be surprised if they jump – especially if ticklish!)
6. If the action is not properly completed by any one or all of the three players, or if any one of the three forgets or makes the wrong move, then 'it' takes their place in the circle and the player who made the error comes into the middle of the circle.

VARIATIONS: Choose more than one player to be in the centre.

SOURCE: Donna Brandes

LAUGHTER IS THE BEST MEDICINE

AIMS: To have fun and reap all the benefits of enjoying laughter in a group.

MATERIALS: None.

PROCEDURE:
1. Everyone stands in a circle.
2. Any group member may start, by making a noise, saying something, making a movement, or any combination of these, in an attempt to make the others laugh.
3. The person to the right copies the noise, action or movement, and this carries on around the circle.
4. If any member laughs or smiles, they must sit down and drop out temporarily.
5. Anyone left standing may begin the next round.

VARIATIONS: The action could be non-verbal, or, in a foreign language (real or imaginary). Use impressions or mannerisms of famous people, e.g. Jim Carey.

NOTES: Discuss with group members the healing power of laughter, tears, or the expression of feelings in general.

SOURCE: Donna Brandes
John Norris

MUNCHY MOMENTS

AIMS: Sharing, listening, similarities and differences.

MATERIALS: None.

PROCEDURE:
1. Everyone closes their eyes and thinks back to their early memories about food.
2. The leader asks them to think of some of their favourites – things their mother (or whoever did the cooking) made for them – concentrating on the feelings they had when they were enjoying those foods.
3. Next, the group think of horrible things that they hated, and were perhaps forced to eat, and concentrate on the feelings that went with this.
4. There is group discussion about these pleasant and unpleasant memories. Group members also discuss whether food is important to them or not, and if so, how it influences their lives.
5. Lastly, everyone should role-play dinner table scenes from their past, perhaps preparing plays in small groups.

VARIATIONS: Show videos of famous food films like, *Eat, Drink, Man, Woman*, or *Willie Wonka and the Chocolate Factory*, depending on the ages of the players. Continue discussions about the importance of food in our lives. In Home Economics, you could discuss diet and nutrition. People could make a huge mural or model of all their favourite and detested foods.

SOURCE: Kerys Murrell

MY NAME GAME

AIMS: Learning names permanently and quickly.

MATERIALS: None.

PROCEDURE:
1. The leader starts a round where each person talks about their name.
2. The leader says that the participants can talk about their names, explaining what it means, where they got it from, why their parents chose it, and how they feel about it. Participants must be sure to mention their name – the one they want to be called by in the group – several times in their speech, so that they reinforce it in the group's minds.
3. The leader starts, modelling an example using their own name, e.g. "My name is Sally, but I was originally called Sarah. I am not exactly sure what Sarah means, but I think it is very biblical, and I have been told it means Princess. My parents called me Sarah, but my little sister could not say that, so she called me Sarly, which we changed to Sally. At school I was always Sally, and now that I am grown-up, well I thought of going back to my original name, but I am so 'Sally' inside now, and I like the image it gives me, that I have always kept it as Sally."

VARIATIONS: Choose a new name for the duration of the group session, play the game again, and issue name tags with the new names on them.

NOTES: If other people know the meaning of a name, they can say it after the round is over.

SOURCE: Donna Brandes

Select Bibliography

Brandes, Donna *The Hope Street Experience*, Access Publishing, 1981

Brandes, Donna and Phillips, Howard *Gamesters' Handbook, 140 Games for Teachers and Group Leaders*, Stanley Thornes (Publishers) Ltd, 1990

Brandes, Donna *Gamesters' Handbook Two*, Stanley Thornes (Publishers) Ltd, 1990

Brandes, Donna and Ginnis, Paul *The Student-Centred School*, UK, Simon and Schuster, 1992

Brandes, Donna and Ginnis, Paul *A Guide to Student-Centred Learning*, UK, Simon and Schuster, 1994

Chapman, Judith, *et all*, *Improving the Quality of Australian Schools*, The Australian Council for Educational Research Ltd.

Covey, Stephen R. *The 7 Habits of Highly Effective People, Powerful Lessons in Personal Change*, New York, Fireside, 1990

Davis, Kathy *A Light Heart Lives Long*, Victoria, Brolga Publishing Pty Ltd, 1990

Harris, Frank W. *Games*, Self published, 1982

Holt, John *How Children Fail*, London, Penguin Books, 1984

Holt, John *How Children Learn*, London, Penguin Books, 1984

Jones, Ken *Designing Your Own Simulations*, London and New York, Methuen, 1985

Munby, Stephen *Assessing & Recording Achievement*, Oxford, Basil Blackwell, 1989

Neelands, Jonothan *Making Sense of Drama, A Guide to Classroom Practice*, Oxford, Heinemann Educational Books, 1984

Newby, Peter *The giant Book of Word Games*, Sydney, The Book Company, 1996

Neville, Bernie *Educating Psyche*, Blackburn, Victoria, Collins Dove , 1989

Renfield, Richard *If Teachers Were Free*, New York, Dell Publishing Co., Inc, 1971

Rogers, Carl *Client-Centred Therapy*, Boston, Houghton–Muffin, 1951

Rogers, Carl *Freedom to learn in the Eighties*, Boston, Houghton–Muffin, 1983

Settle, Davis and Wise, Charles *Choices*, Oxford, Basil Blackwell, 1982

Skynner & Cleese *Life and How to Survive it*, London, Methuen, 1993

Weinstein, Gerald and Fantini, Mario D. *Toward Humanistic Education A Curriculum of Affect*, New York, Praeger Publishers, 1970

List of Games

† denotes 'unpacked' game